CAMPAIGN 273

POINT PLEASANT 1774

Prelude to the American Revolution

JOHN F WINKLER

ILLUSTRATED BY PETER DENNIS
Series editor Marcus Cowper

Editorial by Ilios Publishing Ltd, Oxford, UK (www.iliospublishing.com)
Index by Mark Swift
Typeset in Myriad Pro and Sabon
Maps by Bounford.com
3D bird's-eye view by The Black Spot
Battlescene illustrations by Peter Dennis
Originated by PDQ Media, Bungay, UK
Printed in China through Worldprint Ltd.

14 15 16 17 18   10 9 8 7 6 5 4 3 2 1

ACKNOWLEDGMENTS

The author's old Wellston friends Eleanor Essman, Mike Martin, Red Martin, Mike Murdoch, and Tom Walton roamed the hills of southeastern Ohio finding site photographs. Ed Lowe provided pictures from his vast collection of Point Pleasant photographs, Dale Benington from his unrivaled collection of 18th-century site photographs, and Jeff Dearth pictures of objects in his remarkable collection of early artifacts. Louise Tilzey-Bates, Alexandra Deckerf, Rick Robol, and Wendy S. Winkler took other photographs. Craig Hesson offered valuable information on the sequence and locations of events during the battle. John Baker led the author through the Point Pleasant woods to sites that are seldom seen. Gerald Argabright and Bill Harsha guided him to Pickaway Plains sites that usually are inaccessible. Jack Fowler, John Sauer, Martha Fout and Ruth Fout aided him in finding information on the battle.

ARTIST'S NOTE

Readers may care to note that the original paintings from which the colour plates in this book were prepared are available for private sale. The Publishers retain all reproduction copyright whatsoever. All enquiries should be addressed to:

Peter Dennis, Fieldhead, The Park, Mansfield, Notts, NG18 2AT
magie.h@ntlworld.com

The Publishers regret that they can enter into no correspondence upon this matter.

THE WOODLAND TRUST

Osprey Publishing are supporting the Woodland Trust, the UK's leading woodland conservation charity, by funding the dedication of trees.

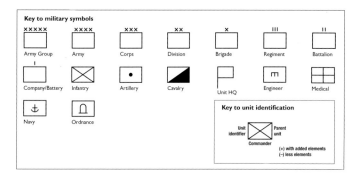

CONTENTS

British North America in 1774

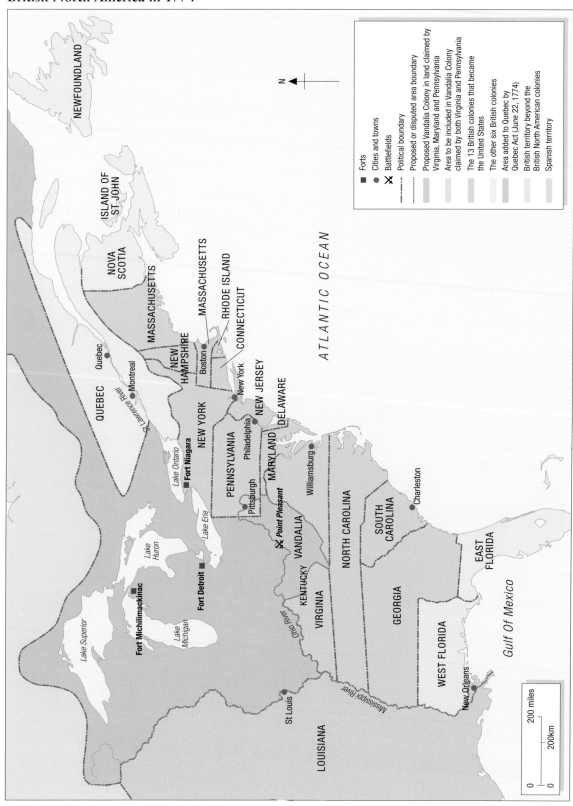

Legend

- ■ Forts
- ● Cities and towns
- ✕ Battlefields
- Political boundary
- Proposed or disputed area boundary
- Proposed Vandalia Colony in land claimed by Virginia, Maryland and Pennsylvania
- Area to be included in Vandalia Colony claimed by both Virginia and Pennsylvania
- The 13 British colonies that became the United States
- The other six British colonies
- Area added to Quebec by Quebec Act (June 22, 1774)
- British territory beyond the British North American colonies
- Spanish territory

NEWFOUNDLAND

ISLAND OF ST JOHN

NOVA SCOTIA

MASSACHUSETTS

MASSACHUSETTS

RHODE ISLAND

NEW HAMPSHIRE

CONNECTICUT

ATLANTIC OCEAN

Quebec

Montreal

St Lawrence River

QUEBEC

Boston

New York

NEW JERSEY

DELAWARE

Lake Ontario

Fort Niagara

NEW YORK

PENNSYLVANIA

Philadelphia

MARYLAND

Lake Erie

Pittsburgh

✕ Point Pleasant

Williamsburg

VANDALIA

Charleston

NORTH CAROLINA

Lake Huron

KENTUCKY

SOUTH CAROLINA

Fort Detroit

Lake Superior

Fort Michilimackinac

Lake Michigan

VIRGINIA

Ohio River

GEORGIA

EAST FLORIDA

Gulf Of Mexico

WEST FLORIDA

New Orleans

Mississippi River

St Louis

LOUISIANA

N

200 miles

200km

0

0

INTRODUCTION

In 1774, the people in 13 of Britain's North American colonies were on the brink of rebellion. War then erupted west of the Appalachians between Britain's greatest colony, Virginia, and the Mingo and Shawnee Indians of what is now Ohio. As George Washington and other Virginia delegates traveled to Philadelphia to attend the first Continental Congress, John Murray, 4th Earl of Dunmore, the last royal governor of the colony, led more than 2,400 other Virginians against the Indians.

In what would be remembered as Lord Dunmore's War, two Virginia militia armies invaded Ohio. Dunmore led one and his American subordinate, Col. Andrew Lewis, the other. Many of the officers and men in the armies would become famous figures of the Revolutionary War and frontier history.

On October 10, 1774, about 700 Indians attacked Lewis's 1,100-man army. The victory of the Virginians at the battle of Point Pleasant, which opened Kentucky to American settlement, allowed the independent United States to include what are now the states of West Virginia, Kentucky, Ohio, Indiana, Illinois, Michigan, and Wisconsin within its boundaries after the Revolutionary War.

THE STRATEGIC SITUATION

In 1774, Britain was the world's pre-eminent power. The population of Britain, about 10 million, included a million Scots, one-third of a million Welsh, and 7 million English, whose numerical and cultural predominance was so great that Britain was often known as England. In British Ireland, there were about 1.5 million native, Catholic Irish and a half-million Protestant immigrants. Across the Atlantic, Britain had 19 North American colonies. Although six had few inhabitants, the 13 that stretched down the Atlantic coast from Massachusetts to Georgia had a population of about 2.6 million.

Britain's supremacy followed its victory over France in the French and Indian War. That conflict, known in

In 1749, a French expedition left lead plates at six points along the Allegheny and Ohio rivers to claim the land drained by the rivers and their tributaries for France. This plate was left on August 20, 1749, at the mouth of the Kanawha River. (Virginia Historical Society)

From 1745 to 1752, George Croghan was the leading British trader in the Ohio Country. In 1749, he probably built this stone structure as part of a trading post near present Isleta, Ohio. (Author's photograph)

Europe as the Seven Years War, arose from rival French and British attempts to control the Ohio Country, the area that is now western Pennsylvania, West Virginia, Ohio, Indiana, and Kentucky. The French first tried to stop the activities of men like the British trader George Croghan. On June 1, 1752, Ojibwe and Ottawa Indians, allied with the French, destroyed the most important center of British trade in the Ohio Country, Pickawillany, a Miami Indian village on the Miami River.

The French then began building forts to guard the area, including Fort Duquesne at present-day Pittsburgh. In 1754, George Washington led a colonial militia force to stop the construction. Attacked on July 3, 1754 by a larger French and Indian army, Washington's 400 militiamen were forced to surrender to the French at a small British fortress, Fort Necessity.

Washington's army at Fort Necessity included militia companies led by Andrew Lewis and Adam Stephen. This reproduction of the crude fort is at Fort Necessity National Battlefield, near Farmington, Pa. (Author's collection)

In the war that followed, the Indians of the Ohio Country fought as French allies. Their prowess in combat in the western woods then defied British efforts to defeat them. They destroyed British armies at Monongahela on July 9, 1755 and Grant's Defeat on September 14, 1758. An advance by Gen. John Forbes in 1758 forced the French to evacuate Fort Duquesne. The British were otherwise unable to invade the area.

British victory at the battle of the Plains of Abraham on September 13, 1759, however, denied use of the St Lawrence River to the French. Unable to supply their western outposts, they surrendered their Ohio Country forts to Britain in 1760. In 1763, they acknowledged loss of all of France's North American territory.

In the Royal Proclamation of 1763, the British government announced that, until further notice, the Ohio Country would be left to the Indians, traders, and the garrisons of the British forts. Any further colonial

settlement there was banned. But the Ohio Indians, led by the Ottawa chief Pontiac, nonetheless decided to renew the war that France had lost. On May 16, 1763, they captured by deceit British Fort Sandusky in northern Ohio, and on July 31 defeated a British force at Bloody Run. They were unable, however, to take the main British strongholds in the west, Fort Detroit and Fort Pitt, which the British had built at the site of Fort Duquesne. They also failed to destroy a force sent to relieve Fort Pitt. On August 5–6, 1763, about 200 Indians attacked 500 men led by Col. Henry Bouquet at Bushy Run. There the brilliant Bouquet saved his army from annihilation by devising a feigned retreat and bayonet charge by concealed soldiers.

These re-enactors are at the site of Bouquet's victory, now Bushy Run Battlefield, near Harrison City, Pa. (Photography by Amanda Wilson)

In 1764, when Bouquet and Maj. Gen. John Bradstreet invaded Ohio with much larger armies, the Indians ended Pontiac's War without further battle. The interest of the British government in the Ohio Country then waned. Except for Forts Michilimackinac, Detroit, and Niagara, the British began abandoning their strongholds west of the Appalachians.

Sir William Johnson, the adopted Mohawk who served as British Superintendent of Indian Affairs for the northern colonies, then labored to avoid any further Indian wars. In Pittsburgh, a village that had arisen at the site of Fort Pitt, Croghan served as Johnson's deputy. There he oversaw relations with the Ohio Indians with his assistant, the Shawnee Alexander McKee.

Because of wars between the Indians, that part of the Ohio Country south of the Ohio River was uninhabited. There, in present-day West Virginia and Kentucky, only hunters and war parties roamed. The Iroquois of New York, a confederacy of the Mohawk, Oneida, Onondaga, Cayuga, and Seneca tribes, claimed dominion over the area. So did their enemies the Cherokee of Tennessee and Georgia. In 1768, a British attempt to obtain the land for settlement succeeded. The Iroquois sold their claim in the Treaty of Fort Stanwix, and the Cherokee in the Treaty of Lochaber.

Virginia claimed all, and Pennsylvania part, of the area as within their colonies' borders. But in 1769, the British government approved a proposal to create a new North American colony in the area, Vandalia. From the new colony's capital, at the mouth of the Kanawha River, its government would rule the area that is now southwestern Pennsylvania, West Virginia, and eastern Kentucky.

In 1770, Johnson was able to make the proposed colony safer for settlement by negotiating peace between the Iroquois and Cherokee. The prospects for attracting settlers to Vandalia then appeared bright. Since the outbreak of the French and Indian War, the population of the British colonies in North America had more than doubled. The largest American town, Philadelphia, had about 35,000 people. New York, Boston, and Charleston followed, with populations of about 25,000, 16,000, and 12,000.

To visitors from London, which in 1774 had nearly a million people, such places appeared prosperous but unimpressive. To them, the American colonies resembled very provincial areas of England. From Boston to Charleston, bewigged gentlemen and gowned ladies presided over political and social affairs of only local importance. Around them lived men and women of humbler status, who ranged in states of respectability from flourishing farmers and tradesmen to servants and black slaves.

To prevail in the French and Indian War, Britain had incurred a crippling debt. To the financially pressed British, it seemed fair that the American colonists should share the cost. The British government therefore had legislated that the Americans must buy imported goods only from Britain, and pay a variety of special taxes.

The colonists responded to the legislation with an outrage that bewildered the British. They had often quarreled with one another. Colonial border disagreements had sometimes even led to armed conflicts. From 1732 through 1736, Marylanders led by Thomas Cresap had battled Pennsylvanians in a dispute ultimately resolved by the Mason–Dixon Line. But now anger united the Americans. A government in London, elected by men who lived across the Atlantic, appeared to recognize no limit to its power over them. It had, moreover, stationed an army of more than 7,000 soldiers in the colonies. On December 16, 1773, men destroyed tea on ships in Boston harbor to protest against one of the new taxes. As 1774 began, the colonists nervously awaited news of what the British response to the Boston Tea Party would be.

THE APPALACHIAN FRONTIER

Few visitors from London ever followed the rough roads and horse trails that led west toward the Appalachian Mountains. As late as 1720, the colonists had all lived within 100 miles of the Atlantic coast. Then British immigrants of a different kind had begun to arrive. Their medieval ancestors had lived on the border between Scotland and England, where the march lords had warred, and raiding had been a way of life. In the late 16th century, many had begun migrating to Ireland, where these Protestant newcomers had fought the native, Catholic Irish in the bitter wars of Elizabeth I, Cromwell, and William of Orange.

About 1720, some began arriving in America, where they would be known as the Scotch-Irish. In the main colonial towns, where their customs marked them as aliens, they found a frigid welcome. Most, moreover, like two-thirds of all immigrants to America, had paid for their passage by selling themselves to ships' captains as indentured servants. Auctioned off in the Atlantic ports, they became, in effect, slaves with fixed dates of emancipation. During their servitude, which lasted as long as six years, their fates depended upon the benevolence of their purchasers. Some were well treated.

Others were beaten or even kept in chains. When their terms of servitude ended, they wanted, above all, lives in which they and their children would not be the servants of others.

The Scotch-Irish, and other immigrants who joined them, left the existing colonial towns and farms with instruments of independence: axes to build homesteads and clear fields, and firearms to hunt and defend themselves. They followed first an Indian path, the Iroquois War Trail, which they widened into the Great Wagon Road. It led from Pennsylvania to the Shenandoah River Valley in Virginia, and on through the headwaters of the James and New rivers. The most venturesome followed Indian trails along the Holston River to what is now Tennessee, and through the western range of the Appalachians into what are now southwestern Pennsylvania, western Maryland, and West Virginia.

There these vigorous and self-reliant people settled, often tens of miles from their nearest neighbors. Those who complied with their colony's land laws had their sites surveyed, and took the maps to the nearest towns for recording. If no rival claimants objected within six months, the land was theirs. Others just demonstrated their claims by blazing on tree trunks the outer limits of their domains.

They found danger on the frontier. In 1742, 28 Iroquois warriors, returning from an expedition against the Catawbas in South Carolina, killed the cattle of settlers living near the James River. When 35 settlers confronted them on December 19, 1742, the encounter ended in battle. Eleven settlers and eight Iroquois died at McDowell's Fight. Payment of compensation to

In 1763, 19-year-old Ann Bailey emigrated to Virginia as an indentured servant. When her husband fell at Point Pleasant, she became a famous scout and Indian fighter. This engraving from Henry Howe's 1848 Historical Collections of Ohio preserves a sketch of her by an anonymous 18th-century artist. The celebrated frontierswoman is buried at Tu-Endie Wei/Point Pleasant Battlefield State Park. (Author's Collection)

The prisoners taken by Chartier's warriors in 1744 included 12-year-old Catherine Cougar. After five years of slavery in a Shawnee village on the Pickaway Plains, she was sold to French traders and ultimately returned to Pennsylvania. When she emigrated with her son to Ohio in 1798, she discovered that the land he had purchased was the site of the village. This monument is at the site. (Photograph by Dale Benington)

the Iroquois by Virginia then ended the threat of war. Then, in 1744, the Shawnee chief Peter Chartier led a small band of warriors in raids against the frontier settlers to aid the French during King George's War. Such conflicts with Indians, however, were rare. The Pennsylvania, Maryland, and Virginia colonists had not experienced war with the Indians since 1677.

But in 1755 the French persuaded the Ohio Indians to attack the western settlers in the French and Indian War. Neither British soldiers nor colonial militiamen could protect them from the onslaught. The terrorized settlers abandoned whole counties in their flight to refugee camps on the Atlantic coast.

But these descendants of many generations of warriors soon learned how to defend themselves. In 1756, they still sang in Scotland the ballad "Johnnie Armstrong," the tale of a fierce border raider who had died in about 1530. In the only success of the British in battling the Ohio Indians during the French and Indian War, his descendant John Armstrong led 300 Pennsylvania frontiersmen against Kittanning, a large Delaware village on the Allegheny River. On September 8, 1756, they surprised its 50 defenders, killed 20, and freed 11 captives.

When Indian raiding ended in 1760, the frontier settlers returned to their abandoned homesteads. In 1763, when Pontiac's warriors appeared with no warning, the flight from the frontier recurred. But after the end of Pontiac's War, the settlers advanced again. In the north, they followed British military roads built during the French and Indian War. Forbes Road led to Pittsburgh from Carlisle, Pa., and Braddock's from Winchester, Va. Burd's Road led on from Braddock's Road to Redstone Old Fort, an Indian ruin on the Monongahela. To the south, from Braddock's Road, they followed McCulloch's Path, a trail blazed by the trader William McCulloch to the Monongahela; and the Warriors' Path and Shawnee Path, Indian trails that led to what is now Elkins, W. Va. Still farther south, from the Great Wagon Road, they followed the Kanawha Trail, which led toward the Ohio River; and the Ingles Ferry Road and Indian trails that led down the Holston River to Tennessee. By 1774, the westernmost were at frontier strongholds like Ebenezer Zane's Blockhouse at what is now Wheeling, W. Va.; Joseph Tomlinson's Fort at Moundsville; Zackwell Morgan's Fort at Morgantown; Daniel Davisson's Fort at Clarksburg; Walter Kelly's Station at Cedar Grove; William Russell's Fort at Castlewood, Va.; and Evan Shelby's Fort at Bristol, Tennessee.

Such settlements were in theory in the westernmost counties of the existing colonies. But some on the frontier didn't know even what colony they were in. In 1772, Shelby and his neighbors, unsure whether they were in Virginia or North Carolina, formed their own government, the Watauga Association.

The western settlers also had little respect for royal authority. Afraid after Pontiac's War that the Indians soon would attack again, they watched in anger as traders carried munitions west to replenish the Indians' supplies. In 1765, James Smith, who had lived as an adopted Mingo for four years, organized a band of Pennsylvania settlers to interdict the trade. At the request of the traders, the commandant at British Fort Loudoun sent soldiers who arrested some of them. Smith and 300 men then besieged the fort for two days. On November 11, 1765, the British released the prisoners. When the commandant at Fort Bedford took similar action in 1769, Smith again saved

The Appalachian Frontier

Map legend:

Forbes Road
Braddock's Road
Burd's Road
Great Wagon Road
Ingles Ferry Road
McCulloch's Path
Warriors' Path
Shawnee Path
Kanawha Trail
Wilderness Trail
Horse Trails
Lewis 1756 Expedition
Bouquet 1764 Expedition

Colony boundaries
Disputed area boundaries
Colony county boundaries

American colonial towns
Estates
Abandoned British forts
Settlers' forts and stations
Battles
Other sites

Map labels:

Beaver River, ✗ Kittanning, WESTMORELAND, Allegheny River, PENNSYLVANIA, Fort Pitt, Hannastown, AREA DISPUTED BY PENNSYLVANIA AND VIRGINIA, ☐ Fort Ligonier, BEDFORD, Carlisle, William Crawford's Fort, Ebenezer Zane's Blockhouse, Redstone Old Fort, Fort Bedford, OTHER PENNSYLVANIA COUNTIES, Fort Loudoun, Ohio River, Monongahela River, Zackwell Morgan's Fort, Fort Cumberland, MARYLAND, BERKELEY, Potomac River, West Fork River, QUEBEC, Daniel Davisson's Fort, HAMPSHIRE, FREDERICK, Winchester, Greenway Court, Little Kanawha River, AUGUSTA, DUNMORE, Shenandoah River, Point Pleasant ✗, VIRGINIA, CULPEPER, BOTETOURT, Greenbrier River, Walter Kelly's Station, Kanawha River, Staunton, Fort Lewis Plantation, Big Sandy River, FINCASTLE, James River, KENTUCKY, ✗ McDowell's Fight, Andrew Lewis's Fort, Belmont, OTHER VIRGINIA COUNTIES, Smithfield Plantation, BEDFORD, N, Ingles Ferry, William Russell's Fort, New River, Cumberland Gap, Evan Shelby's Fort, Holston River, Watauga River, NORTH CAROLINA

0 — 50 miles
0 — 50km

the arrested men. At dawn on September 12, 1769, he and 18 men rushed the fort when the gates opened. After freeing the prisoners, they allowed its 30 soldiers to resume their garrison duties. Fort Bedford, Smith later wrote, "was the first British fort in America that was taken by what they called 'American rebels.'"

By 1774, about 30,000 settlers lived on the Appalachian frontier in centers of population such as Pittsburgh, which had 40 log cabins; in small fortresses like Doddridge's Blockhouse near present Washington, Pa.; and on scattered homesteads. In their world, poverty seemed a natural condition of life. Eight-year-old Lewis Doddridge, sent to school in Baltimore in 1777, later wrote, "When I arrived there I was in a new world. I had left the

The photograph shows reconstructed Fort Loudoun at Fort Loudoun State Historic Site in Fort Loudon, Pa. (Courtesy of the Fort Loudon Historical Society)

backwoods behind me. I had exchanged its rough manners and poor living for the buildings, plenty and polish of civilized life."

But on the frontier, freedom also seemed as natural as poverty. In Baltimore, sights that "were viewed with indifference by the whole population of the neighborhood, as matters of course" shocked Doddridge. While returning from school one day, he saw a rich neighbor whip a servant. "I went home with a heavy heart," he recalled, "and wished myself in the backwoods again."

THE OHIO INDIANS

From about 1660 until 1701, the Ohio Country had been uninhabited. The conflicts known as the Beaver Wars, in which the Iroquois had battled Indians as far west as the Mississippi River, made the Ohio Country too dangerous for habitation. But after 1701, when the Treaty of Montreal ended the Beaver Wars, the part of the Ohio Country north and west of the Ohio River began to be repopulated.

By 1774, about 20,000 people lived in the area. By birth or adoption, most were members of the Delaware, Kickapoo, Miami, Mingo, Ojibwe, Ottawa, Potawatomi, or Wyandot Indian tribes. But the Beaver Wars and their aftermath had changed the composition of such tribes forever. Decades of life as refugees among once hostile groups had blurred traditional genetic distinctions. Interaction with French and British traders, soldiers, and captives had left changes that sometimes were visible. There were blond Delawares and black Shawnees. Intermarriage also had altered the nature of tribal loyalties. Many Ohio Indian children had parents who belonged to different tribes. Some Indians cared little for traditional tribal identities and customs. All were fiercely independent.

On the Tuscarawas River, there were Christian Delaware villages, where Indians converted by Moravian missionaries lived much like the colonial settlers. But elsewhere, the Indians passed their years as they had for centuries. In winter they dispersed to hunting lodges and camps, from which the men searched for enough game to avoid starvation. During other seasons,

Indian villages had bark-covered structures like these at George Rogers Clark Memorial Park, near Springfield, Ohio, the site of the battle of Peckuwe on August 8, 1780. (Author's photograph)

they lived in villages like those of the Shawnee on the Pickaway Plains, a level area on the Scioto River.

Visitors to such villages in 1774 first passed large cornfields, where women, children, and slaves labored while the men hunted, warred, or met in councils. Then they saw among the village's traditional bark-covered structures sights that had been unknown to the Indians' ancestors. But from some other sights visitors often averted their eyes. There were displays of the scalps of enemies killed by the village's raiding warriors; 200–300yd-long cleared paths, where captured enemies ran the gauntlet between lines of Indians, trying to evade their captors' clubs and sticks as their fate was decided. And there were posts where captives were tortured and burned to death.

From the villages, narrow trails passed through the woods in every direction. Some led to trading posts like those of the French trader Peter Loramie on Loramie Creek, and the British trader Richard Butler on the Scioto River, where Indians traded in furs and hides at prices fixed by Sir William Johnson. Others led long distances to the south, the routes of raiding warriors in search of scalps, prisoners, and horses.

The trails to the northeast led to the villages of the Iroquois in northwestern Pennsylvania and western New York. When the Ohio Indians had begun emigrating to the Ohio Country about 1720, they had settled on land claimed by the Iroquois, whose permission they had received. Then the Iroquois had sent viceroys known as "Half-kings," to live among the

Thousands of miles of Indian trails, often invisible to untrained eyes, led through the Ohio Country. Some of the main paths, passable on horseback, have been given modern names such as the Kanawha Trail. This marker in Jackson is on the trail's route between Lewis's 3rd and 4th Ohio Camps. (Photograph by Eleanor Essman)

Wyandots and Delaware, men like Shikellany, the father of the Mingo John Logan.

But the power of the Iroquois had waned. When Johnson had asked them to send war parties against the Ohio Indians to end Pontiac's War, few had responded. By 1768, when the Iroquois sold the area east and south of the Ohio River to the British, the Ohio Indians no longer felt themselves bound by any action of the once powerful confederacy.

The sale at Fort Stanwix most directly affected the Shawnee, who had hunted south of the Ohio for decades. When British surveyors began appearing there in 1770, the alarmed Shawnee sent emissaries to the other Ohio Indians; to the Seneca, with whom Johnson had the least influence; and to the Cherokees, Chickasaws, Choctaws, and Creeks in the south. They together, the Shawnee proposed, should renew Pontiac's War on a larger scale, with attacks on the settlements of every colony from New York to Georgia.

In 1771 and 1772, the Shawnee continued their efforts to create a grand alliance. Croghan, however, and McKee, who in 1771 succeeded him as Johnson's deputy, were able to thwart their designs. The Ohio Indians, McKee told the Shawnee in 1773, should welcome the Vandalia Colony instead of opposing it. Soon there would be a colonial government at the mouth of the Kanawha. Unlike the distant governments of Pennsylvania, Maryland, and Virginia, it could not ignore their interests, and would have to regulate settlement effectively.

The Shawnee chiefs found McKee's argument persuasive. But many warriors were unmoved. Even if they could not attack in tribal war parties, independent groups of warriors could make the land south of the Ohio River an area that colonial surveyors and settlers would find too dangerous to enter.

LORD DUNMORE'S VIRGINIA

In 1774, Virginia was by far the most important of Britain's North American colonies. Its population, about 600,000, was twice that of its nearest rivals, Pennsylvania and Massachusetts. Ruled by a royal governor, the colony had 57 counties. In each, the free, adult males constituted the local militia, and selected two county representatives for the colony's legislature, the House of Burgesses.

On September 25, 1771, John Murray, the 4th Earl of Dunmore, became the new governor of Virginia. The Scottish lord's star had begun to rise in 1768, when his wife's sister had married the politically powerful Granville Leveson-Gower, the 2nd Earl Gower. Gower, who later would become the 1st Marquess of Stafford, had obtained the royal appointment for him.

Dunmore soon met the colony's richest resident, Thomas Fairfax, Baron Fairfax of Cameron. Fairfax had made his fortune investing in land in Virginia. From his new friend, the avaricious Dunmore learned that the best land investments were now in the vast area west of the Appalachians that Virginia claimed as within the colony's borders.

During the French and Indian War, the colony had raised the Virginia Regiment, a uniformed unit minimally trained to fight with British regulars. To pay the cost of their years of service, Virginia had promised each soldier 50 acres of the western land, and the officers tracts as large as 5,000 acres.

When the 1768 sales by the Iroquois and Cherokee opened the area for settlement, Washington asked the Virginia government to honor the promises by authorizing a survey of tracts for veterans between the mouths of the Little Kanawha and Kanawha rivers on the Ohio, and up the Kanawha. In 1770, he and his friend William Crawford, guided by McKee, spent a month surveying the best sites for settlement.

But there were many other potential settlement sites, especially in the area known as Kentucky. Investments in the most desirable, Dunmore thought, could in time create a fortune beyond the dreams of even the richest London lords and merchants. The Virginia governor began his speculation by acquiring from the colony 100,000 acres at the falls of the Ohio River, the site of present Louisville.

Two obstacles, however, stood in the way of the Virginia governor's plan to emulate Fairfax. The first was the proposed Vandalia Colony, which would include the land that Dunmore had obtained from Virginia. At his brother-in-law's request, Gower took action to block the Vandalia Colony project. The second was Pennsylvania. Virginia's western lands could be reached most easily by the Ohio River, which led southwest from Pittsburgh. Both Pennsylvania and Virginia claimed the area around Pittsburgh as within their borders. Pennsylvania, however, was already administering it.

"If that man is not crushed," Washington wrote of Dunmore after the outbreak of the Revolutionary War in 1775, "he will become the most formidable enemy America has." This 1929 copy by Charles X. Harris of a 1765 portrait by Sir Joshua Reynolds depicts Dunmore in the highland dress of the 3rd Regiment of Foot Guards (now the Scots Guards). (Virginia Historical Society)

Previously part of Bedford County, on February 26, 1773, the area had become part of new Westmoreland County, with its seat of government at the village of Hannastown. In the new county, the great landowner Arthur St Clair acted as local agent for Thomas Penn, the governor of Pennsylvania. Crawford was one of its three judges. James Smith was one of its three commissioners, elected to administer the new county's affairs. Croghan, a leading proponent of the Vandalia Company; his nephew, the ambitious John Connolly; and McKee were other important Westmoreland County figures, and also the prominent Indian traders Richard Butler, John Gibson, and Matthew Elliott.

He must, Dunmore concluded, press his colony's claim to the Pittsburgh area immediately so that Gower could have the British government decide the dispute in Virginia's favor. To obtain support for Virginia's claim from the local population, Dunmore recruited Connolly. He, in turn, enlisted the aid of the able Indian trader Simon Girty, who had lived as a Mingo for eight years.

In December, 1773, Dunmore learned that Gower had succeeded in halting the Vandalia Colony project. He then took bold action to ensure that Virginia's claim would be addressed quickly. He sent Connolly to Pittsburgh with orders to form a rival Virginia government. As Connolly rode up Braddock's Road, he stopped at Crawford's Fort, where he told his host that the Vandalia Colony project had been canceled. "Connolly called on me on his way from Williamsburg," a puzzled Crawford wrote to Washington, "and tells me that it is now without doubt that the new government is fallen through and that Lord Dunmore is to take charge of so much of this quarter as falls out of Pennsylvania." When Connolly reached Pittsburgh on January 6, he posted an announcement on the gate of abandoned Fort Pitt that the area now was the Western District of Augusta County, Virginia. As "Captain, Commandant of the Militia of Pittsburgh and its Dependencies," he ordered the local militiamen to assemble there on January 25.

Dunmore gave little thought to a third possible obstacle. Although war between the Ohio Indians and the settlers had ended in 1764, there since had been incidents in which Indians and settlers had died. Three months before, there had been an especially disturbing one.

On September 25, 1773, Daniel Boone and his friend William Russell, who would lead a company at Point Pleasant, began to assemble a party of 100 settlers, who planned to establish the first settlement in Kentucky. On October 9, Indians attacked 15 of the settlers as they were traveling to join the others. They killed seven, including Boone's and Russell's 17-year-old sons, and took the other eight prisoners. The settlers then abandoned the migration and returned home. When three of the Indians' captives escaped, they identified as one of the attackers the Shawnee warrior Bededee, who had often visited the Boone cabin. Bedeedee, they added, had tortured the wounded Boone and Russell boys before killing them.

When McKee inquired about the incident, the Shawnee chiefs expressed condolences for the deaths, but denied that any Shawnees had been responsible. Although McKee soon learned that Shawnee warriors had been the killers, the response of the chiefs did not surprise him. Like them, he knew that no one could control what individual warriors or settlers might do on the frontier. Such an incident, unless it was overlooked, could easily cause a war.

This Fort Pitt blockhouse, built by Bouquet in 1764, survives near the Fort Pitt Museum in Pittsburgh's Point State Park. (Courtesy of the Senator John Heinz History Center)

CHRONOLOGY

c.1640–1701	Beaver Wars depopulate Ohio Country.
1701–54	Repopulation of Ohio Country.
1754–60	French and Indian War.
1763–64	Pontiac's War.
1768	Iroquois and Cherokee cede Kentucky and West Virginia to Britain.
1770	Washington and Crawford surveying expedition on the Ohio River.
1771	Dunmore appointed governor of Virginia.
December 16, 1773	Boston Tea Party.

1774

January 6	Connolly begins attempt to seize Westmoreland County, Pa., for Virginia.
April 30	Massacre at Baker's trading post.
June 2	British close port of Boston.
June 10	Dunmore orders frontier county lieutenants to assemble militia companies.
August 2	Battle of Wakatomica.
September 5	Commencement of 1st Continental Congress.
September 6	Charles Lewis and Augusta County Regiment leave Camp Union (1st W. Va. Camp) for mouth of Elk River.
September 12	Andrew Lewis and Botetourt County Regiment advance from Camp Union to 2nd W. Va. Camp.

September 13	Lewis reaches 3rd W. Va. Camp.
September 14	Lewis reaches 4th W. Va. Camp.
September 15	Lewis reaches 5th W. Va. Camp.
September 16	Lewis reaches 6th W. Va. Camp.
September 17	Lewis reaches 7th W. Va. Camp.
September 18	Lewis reaches 8th W. Va. Camp.
September 19	Lewis reaches 9th W. Va. Camp.
September 20	Lewis reaches 10th W. Va. Camp.
September 21	Lewis reaches 11th W. Va. Camp.
September 22	Botetourt County Regiment joins Augusta County Regiment at 12th W. Va. Camp. Congress asks American merchants to cease purchasing British goods.
September 27	Christian and Fincastle County Regiment advance from Camp Union.
September 30	Dunmore reaches Wheeling. Lewis's army reaches 13th W. Va. Camp.
October 2	Lewis's army reaches 14th W. Va. Camp.
October 3	Lewis's army reaches 15th W. Va. Camp.
October 4	Lewis's army reaches 16th W. Va. Camp.
October 5	Lewis's army reaches 17th W. Va. Camp.
October 6	Lewis's army reaches 18th W. Va. Camp at Point Pleasant, Fincastle County Regiment reaches Lewis's 12th W. Va. Camp. Dunmore's army reaches mouth of Hocking River.
October 10	Battle of Point Pleasant. Fincastle County Regiment reaches Point Pleasant. Dunmore's army crosses Ohio River to 1st Ohio Camp.
October 11	Dunmore's army reaches 2nd Ohio Camp.
October 12	Dunmore's army reaches 3rd Ohio Camp.
October 13	Dunmore's army reaches 4th Ohio Camp.
October 14	Dunmore's army reaches 5th Ohio Camp. Congress issues Declaration of Colonial Rights.

October 15	Dunmore's army reaches 6th Ohio Camp.
October 17	Dunmore's army reaches 7th Ohio Camp (Camp Charlotte). Lewis's army reaches 1st Ohio Camp.
October 18	Lewis's army reaches 2nd Ohio Camp.
October 19	Lewis's army reaches 3rd Ohio Camp.
October 20	Lewis's army reaches 4th Ohio Camp. Congress votes to create American Association.
October 21	Lewis's army reaches 5th Ohio Camp.
October 22	Lewis's army reaches 6th Ohio Camp.
October 23	Lewis's army reaches 7th Ohio Camp.
October 24	Advance of Lewis's army stopped by Dunmore.
October 25	Lewis's army leaves 7th Ohio Camp. Crawford advances toward Seekunk.
October 26	Congress dissolves with announcement that it will reconvene on May 10, 1775.
October 27	Battle of Seekunk.
October 31	Dunmore's army leaves Camp Charlotte.
November 5	Dunmore's officers agree on Fort Gower Resolves.
December 22	Fort Gower Resolves appears in *Virginia Gazette*.

1775

April 19	Battles of Lexington and Concord.

OPPOSING COMMANDERS

VIRGINIA COMMANDERS

John Murray, 4th Earl of Dunmore, led the Virginia militiamen. Forty-two in 1774, he had been present at the battle of Culloden on April 16, 1746, as a 15-year-old page to the Jacobite pretender Charles Stuart. After later service as a British officer and Royal Governor of New York, he was Royal Governor of Virginia in 1774.

Dunmore's militiamen advanced as two forces, sometimes called his Northern and Southern armies. Units of the Northern Army fought at Wakatomica and Seekunk. Most of the Southern Army fought at Point Pleasant.

Dunmore personally led the Northern Army. His principal subordinates were **Col. Adam Stephen**, the County Lieutenant of Berkeley County; **Maj. Angus McDonald**, who nominally led the Frederick County Regiment; **Maj. William Crawford**, who acted as commander of the Frederick County Regiment; and **Maj. John Connolly**, who led the West Augusta District Battalion.

Stephen, who led the Berkeley County Regiment, had served as second in command of George Washington's Virginia Regiment during the French and Indian War. He would become an American major-general during the Revolutionary War, but his career would end in 1777 in a court martial conviction for commanding while drunk at the battle of Germantown.

McDonald, whose family provided the chieftains of a famous Scottish clan, had fought as an 18-year-old lieutenant for Charles Stuart at Culloden. A major in the Frederick County militia, he led the Wakatomica expedition that preceded Point Pleasant. He then served as a staff officer for Dunmore while nominally commanding the Frederick County Regiment.

Crawford led the Frederick County Regiment, which included McDonald's Wakatomica expedition companies. He also commanded 150 men in the Seekunk expedition that followed Point Pleasant. A close friend of Washington, he would be captured by Indians in 1782 and tortured to death.

In 1774, Adam Stephen lived in a log cabin in what is now Martinsburg, W. Va. In 1778, he replaced it with this house, now a museum in Martinsburg. (Courtesy of the General Adam Stephen Memorial Association, Inc.)

Crawford's company leaders included Capts. **Daniel Morgan** and **George Rogers Clark**. Morgan, who fought at Wakatomica and Seekunk, would be the most brilliant field commander of the Revolutionary War. His stunning victory at Cowpens on January 17, 1781 would be remembered as one of the tactical masterpieces of 18th-century warfare.

Clark, who also fought at Wakatomica and Seekunk, would become the most famous of frontier commanders. His capture of Kaskaskia on July 4, 1778; recapture of Vincennes on February 23, 1779; and victory at the battle of Peckuwe on August 8, 1780 would allow the United States to include within its boundaries after the Revolutionary War what would later become the states of West Virginia, Kentucky, Ohio, Indiana, Illinois, Michigan, and Wisconsin.

Captains **Michael Cresap**, **John Tipton**, and **James Wood** led other companies in Crawford's regiment. Cresap, who also fought at Wakatomica and Seekunk, would join Washington's Continental Army with a rifle company in 1775, but would die later that year. Tipton, who fought at Wakatomica, would lead North Carolina forces against those of Frankland (an independent country in what is now Tennessee that had been established by Lt. John Sevier of the Southern Army) in 1788. Wood, who also fought at Wakatomica, would become a governor of Virginia.

Connolly, Dunmore's principal agent in the area of Pennsylvania occupied by the Virginians, led the West Augusta District Battalion. His company commanders included Capts. **John Gibson** and **George Aston**. Gibson, an adopted Delaware, was the brother-in-law of the Mingo John Logan. He would command Fort Laurens in present Bolivar, Ohio, during the siege by Indians from February 22 to March 20, 1779, and would go on to lead Virginia regiments of the Continental Army, and still later serve as governor of the Indiana territory. His principal subordinate was his brother, Lt. George Gibson, with whom he operated a trading post. George Gibson would die at Wabash on November 4, 1791, commanding the US 2nd Levy Regiment.

Aston fought at Seekunk, where his senior subordinate was Lt. Simon Girty. An adopted Mingo, Girty would become a legendary figure on the Ohio River frontier. After defecting to the British in 1778, he would lead Indian units in raids and battles during the Revolutionary War, and at Wabash.

In 1794, Daniel Morgan sat for this portrait by James Willson Peale dressed in his uniform as a Revolutionary War brigadier-general. (Courtesy of Independence National Historical Park)

After the Revolutionary War, George Rogers Clark settled across the Ohio River from Louisville. The photograph shows the view of the river from the location, now the George Rogers Clark Homesite at Falls of the Ohio State Park in Clarksville, Ind. (Photograph by Historic Southern Indiana)

Dunmore's Northern Army included many other notable officers. Ensign William Oldham would die commanding the Kentucky militiamen at Wabash. Ensign Uriah Springer would lead a battalion of riflemen at the battle of Fallen Timbers on August 20, 1794. Sergeant Ebenezer Zane, the founder of Wheeling, would in 1796 cut across Ohio Zane's Trace, the first horse trail connecting Pennsylvania and Kentucky. Sergeant Robert Benham would be one of two Americans to survive the battle of the Licking River on October 4, 1779. Sergeant Andrew Poe and his brother Adam would on September 18, 1781 conduct a famous rescue of Wyandot captives at Poes' Fight.

Colonel Andrew Lewis, the County Lieutenant of Botetourt County, led the Southern Army. Fifty-four in 1774, Lewis had served as third in command of Washington's Virginia Regiment, fought at Fort Necessity, Monongahela, and Grant's Defeat, led the unsuccessful Big Sandy expedition in 1756, and commanded the Virginians in Bouquet's army in 1764. As a brigadier-general in the Continental Army, with **Adam Stephen** as second in command, he would drive Dunmore from Virginia in 1776. In 1777, he would resign his commission because of illness.

Lewis's staff officers included his Quartermaster-General, **Major Thomas Posey,** whom Washington considered almost a son. After a distinguished career as a brigadier-general in the Revolutionary War, Posey would serve as governor of the Indiana Territory.

Lewis's principal subordinates were his brother **Col. Charles Lewis,** and Cols. **William Fleming, William Christian,** and **John Field.** Charles Lewis, the County Lieutenant of Augusta County, would die at Point Pleasant leading his county's regiment. His company commanders included Capts. **John Lewis, George Matthews,** and **Matthew Arbuckle.** John Lewis was Andrew Lewis's son. Matthews, who would command a regiment during the Revolutionary War, would later serve as governor of Georgia.

Arbuckle, who served as the army's chief guide, would build Fort Randolph at Point Pleasant in 1776, which Indians would besiege in 1777. His principal subordinate was Capt. James Ward, whose small company had been merged into Arbuckle's. Ward, who fell at the battle, was the father of John Ward (White Wolf), an adopted Shawnee who fought with Cornstalk's army at the battle.

Fleming, the colonel of Andrew Lewis's Botetourt County Regiment, would be badly wounded at Point Pleasant. His staff included his Quartermaster-General, Major William Ingles, and his aide-de-camp John Todd. Ingles operated Ingles Ferry, which carried travelers across the New River to the Wilderness Trail. His wife, Mary Draper Ingles, was famous for her celebrated escape from the Shawnees in 1755. Todd, who would be a leading commander of Kentucky militiamen, would die at the battle of Blue Licks on August 19, 1782.

Fleming's captains included **William Russell,** who had tried with Daniel Boone to found a settlement in Kentucky in 1773. His principal subordinate was probably **Lt. John Sevier**. Sevier would win fame as a commander at the battle of King's Mountain on October 7, 1780. He would later serve as governor of the independent country of Frankland, and be the first governor of Tennessee.

Captain Evan Shelby, leader of the independent Watauga Association, led another company in Fleming's unit. Shelby's company, assigned to the Fincastle County Regiment, was attached to Fleming's regiment at the time of Point Pleasant. His principal subordinate was his son **Lt. Isaac Shelby**. During the Revolutionary War, Isaac Shelby would win fame as a commander at King's Mountain. He would later be the first governor of Kentucky, and, during the War of 1812, lead his state's volunteers at the battle of the Thames on October 5, 1813. Sergeant James Robertson of Shelby's company would found Nashville.

Christian, colonel of the Fincastle County Regiment, would lead a successful campaign against the Cherokee in 1776, settle in Kentucky, and be killed by Indians near Louisville in 1785. His wife was Patrick Henry's sister Anne. His company commanders included Capts. William Campbell, James Harrod, and John Floyd. With Shelby and Sevier, Campbell would command the American army at King's Mountain. In 1774, Harrod founded and abandoned the first settlement in Kentucky, to which he would return in 1775. Floyd, one of the most prominent early settlers of Kentucky, would serve as colonel of the Kentucky militia until 1783, when he would be killed in an Indian ambush.

Field, colonel of the Culpeper County Regiment, led three small companies that he recruited for Lewis's army. He fell at Point Pleasant. His subordinates included Sgt. Thomas Barbee, who would command a brigade of 800 Kentucky horsemen at Fallen Timbers.

Other notable officers who fought at Point Pleasant included Augusta County Ensigns John Bowman of Capt. Philip Love's company, and Abraham Lincoln of Capt. Benjamin Harrison's company. In 1779, Bowman would lead the first invasion of Ohio by Kentucky militia forces, an attack on

In 1755, Mary Draper Ingles, the wife of Maj. William Ingles and sister of Lt. John Draper of Capt. Walter Crockett's company, was taken to Lower Shawnee Town at what is now Portsmouth, Ohio, where she spent three months as a slave before escaping. After a 40-day journey across 400 miles of wilderness, she reached safety at a Virginia settlement. In 1762, she and William Ingles settled at Ingles Ferry, near what is now Radford, Va. The photograph shows their reconstructed cabin at Ingles Farm, a historical farm operated by their descendants. (Courtesy of Radford, Va. Visitors Center)

Chalawgatha, near present Xenia. Lincoln, who would lead a company in Gen. Lachlan McIntosh's 1778 invasion of Ohio, would die in an Indian raid in Kentucky in 1786, 23 years before the birth of his namesake, his grandson, the 16th president of the United States.

INDIAN COMMANDERS

The Chalawgatha **Cornstalk** (Hokelesqua), about 55 in 1774, was the Shawnee commander. He had led his people's warriors at Monongahela and Bushy Run, and on many raids into Virginia during the French and Indian and Pontiac's Wars. Cornstalk's Chalawgatha commanders included his brothers **Silver Heels** (Halowas) and **Nimwha**, and **Black Fish** (Chiungalla). An attack on Silver Heels near Pittsburgh caused the Shawnee to decide to fight the Virginians. Nimwha, who commanded the warriors of the Shawnee villages on the Muskingum River, led them in the defense of Wakatomica. Black Fish commanded the warriors from the Chalawgatha village on the Little Miami River.

The grave of Cornstalk at Tu-Endie-Wei/Point Pleasant Battlefield State Park. (Author's photograph)

The Kispoko commanders included **Blue Jacket** (Weyyapiersenwha), **Puckeshinwa**, **Black Snake** (Shemeneto), and **Captain Johnny** (Kekewepelethy). Blue Jacket would command warriors in many engagements during the Revolutionary War, at Wabash, and at Fallen Timbers. Puckeshinwa, who fell at the battle with his 15-year-old son Chiksika, left two notable sons. Six-year-old Tecumseh would become the most famous of Shawnee chiefs. At the time of Puckeshinwa's death, his wife, Methoataske, was pregnant with another son. Known as the Prophet, he would inspire the Indians at the battle of Tippecanoe on November 7, 1811.

The Thawakila **Black Hoof** (Catehecassa) was another Shawnee commander. He would lead the Shawnee at Peckuwe. He would later command the Shawnee who fought as American allies against Tecumseh's Indians at the battle of the Thames.

Pluggy (Plukkekehnote) was the leading Mingo commander at Point Pleasant. Chiefs from other tribes led volunteer units from the Delawares, Wyandots, Ottawas, and Cherokees. The great Delaware commander **Buckongahelas** probably lost an ear at Point Pleasant leading such a unit.

OPPOSING ARMIES

VIRGINIAN FORCES

The Virginians were militiamen in two armies, which each had about 1,400 officers and men. Berkeley, Frederick, and Hampshire counties, and the West Augusta District, provided those in the Northern Army. Augusta, Bedford, Botetourt, Culpeper, Dunmore, and Fincastle counties supplied those in the Southern Army.

In theory, the militia of Virginia counties were organized like those of English counties. Each county had a county lieutenant, who served the same function as an English county's Lord Lieutenant. His militiamen constituted the county regiment, which at full strength had ten companies with 500 men. Its senior officers held permanent commissions as colonels, lieutenant-colonels, and majors. Its junior officers, granted commissions for specific missions, were each company's captain, lieutenant, and two subalterns, who held the rank of ensign and sergeant.

In practice, Virginia militia forces were usually collections of companies raised for specific missions. Prominent men offered to captain companies, and persuaded others to serve in their units as junior officers and privates. During their service, the officers and men received daily compensation from the colony, and men left disabled and women left widowed received pensions or payments.

Militia officers varied in their dress. Those who had served in the Virginia Regiment often wore their colorful uniforms. Some, like Col. Charles Lewis, fell at Point Pleasant, where the Indians targeted them. Others dressed exactly like their men, in the broad-brimmed hats, hunting shirts, leggings, and moccasins worn on the frontier.

Frontier militiamen usually carried their own firearms. By 1774, almost all had what first were known as Pennsylvania rifles.

The costumes of these battle of Point Pleasant re-enactors show the variation in dress of the Virginia militia officers. Eddie Goode (left) wears the uniform of an officer of the Virginia Regiment. Craig Hesson (right), who has a gentleman's tricorn cocked hat, wears a frontier hunting shirt as a light coat over a gentleman's collared shirt. (Photograph by Ed Lowe)

This rifle was used to defend Bryan's Station in Lexington, Ky., in 1782 when Indians led by Simon Girty attacked the stronghold. (Kentucky Historical Society, Mrs Jane Cantrill Collection, 1939.371)

Crafted by men like Richard Butler's father, a gunsmith in Carlisle, Pa., these .32 to .54-cal. weapons were much more accurate than smoothbore muskets. Using powder carried in horns, and balls made from lead bars in molds, most frontiersmen could reload their rifles in about 45 seconds. Marksmen then could hit targets the size of a man at about 200yd.

For close combat, the frontier militiamen used edged weapons. Most carried tomahawks. All carried knives of various types and shapes, most with large or long blades.

Dunmore's militiamen varied in their level of experience. Although most were veterans of battles with Indians, some were young volunteers. Fourteen-year-old Pvt. William Stephen died at Point Pleasant. Fifteen-year-old William Russell, who fought in his father's company, would lead a battalion of Kentucky horsemen at Fallen Timbers and later command the US 17th Infantry Regiment. Sixteen-year-old Martin Wetzel would become a famous frontiersman.

Many of the militiamen would later become celebrated commanders or frontier figures. In the Northern Army, Pvt. John Hardin of Zackwell Morgan's company, who was wounded at Wakatomica, would lead the Kentucky militia in Gen. Josiah Harmar's army at the October 19, 1790 battle known as Hardin's Defeat, and the October 23, 1790 battle of Kekionga. David Williamson of Cresap's company, who fought at Wakatomica and Seekunk, would lead the militiamen who would kill 96 Christian Delaware at the March 9, 1782 Gnadenhutten Massacre. Simon Kenton of Aston's company, who fought at Seekunk, would become a legendary frontier figure. Samuel Wells of Capt. John Stephenson's company would survive Wabash, lead the Kentucky mounted riflemen at Tippecanoe, and later command the US 17th Infantry Regiment. Samuel Mason of the same company would command Fort Henry at Wheeling when it was attacked by Indians in 1777, and later become an Ohio River pirate, terrorizing travelers from a lair at what is now Cave-in-Rock State Park in Illinois. In the Southern Army, James and John Brown of Harrod's company would become important political figures. Second in command of the Kentucky militia at Wabash, James Brown would later serve as US senator from Louisiana and American ambassador to France. John Brown would be a US senator from Kentucky.

His militia, however, did not impress Dunmore. In correspondence he referred to each of his armies as merely a "body of men." The officers, he judged, were incapable of imposing "any order or discipline." The men, he said, were "impressed from their earliest infancy with sentiments and habits very different from those acquired by persons of a similar condition in England." They were, he concluded, "not much less savage" than the Indians.

The muskets and bayonets of British regulars, the Virginia governor knew, would quickly drive an army of such men from an open field. But Dunmore, whose military experience had been in a royal guards regiment in London, had not seen the massacres of British regulars at Monongahela and Grant's Defeat. Battles in the western woods were not for men skilled in fighting in regular formations. They were for men who could fight as irregulars.

By 1774, a century of sobering experiences in Eastern Europe had taught the most astute European commanders the effectiveness of irregulars against regulars in wooded terrain. The great military theorist Maurice de Saxe had concluded that even the strongest regular army formations should have companies of irregular units to combat enemy irregulars.

What looked to Dunmore like parodies of British regular units were instead assemblies of the best irregulars the British empire could produce. His frontier militiamen all had the highest proficiency in use of their firearms. "A well-grown boy, at the age of twelve or thirteen," recalled Lewis Doddridge, "was furnished with a small rifle and pouch... Hunting squirrels, turkeys and raccoons soon made him expert with his gun." They also were masters in use of their edged weapons. "Throwing the tomahawk," Doddridge remembered, "was another boyish sport... A little experience enabled the boy to measure the distance with his eye, when walking through the woods, and strike a tree with his tomahawk in any way he chose."

Combat by irregular forces, which was very difficult for commanders to visualize, required the keenest judgment. Saxe therefore had urged generals to choose their best junior officers as leaders of their irregular units. The quality of Dunmore's and Lewis's commanders was especially critical because of the nature of the men they would lead.

A mistake by an officer commanding the aggressively independent Virginia frontiersmen might easily lead to mutiny or mass desertion. During the Wakatomica expedition, Major Angus McDonald learned how quickly an officer could lose such men's respect. The conduct of 18-year-old Pvt. Abraham Thomas in cleaning a rifle barrel annoyed him. McDonald, Thomas remembered, "came towards me swearing, with an uplifted cane, threatening to strike. I instantly arose on my feet with my rifle barrel in my hand and stood in a position of defense. We looked each other in the eye for some time. At last he dropped his cane and walked off, while the whole troop laughed."

Dunmore's and Lewis's militiamen would also battle the Ohio Indians. The Virginians might aspire to equal, but could not hope to surpass, their skill in conducting irregular operations. "The advantageous way they have of fighting in the woods," Washington wrote, "their cunning and craft, are not to be equalled, nor their activity and indefatigable sufferings."

Dunmore, who never saw his militiamen in combat, believed that their only strength lay in numbers. Far greater British commanders would see

In frontier combat with flintlock rifles, judgment in deciding when to fire and skill in reloading were often as important as marksmanship. Martin Wetzel left behind his 11-year-old brother Lewis at Wetzel's Fort. Lewis Wetzel, who learned to reload a rifle while sprinting, would become a legend among the Indians, who would call him "the Death Wind." This engraving from Wills De Haas's 1851 *History of the Early Settlement and Indian Wars of Western Virginia* shows Lewis Wetzel tricking an Indian into discharging his musket. (Author's Collection)

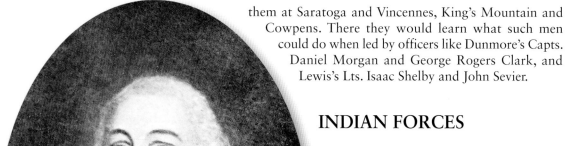

them at Saratoga and Vincennes, King's Mountain and Cowpens. There they would learn what such men could do when led by officers like Dunmore's Capts. Daniel Morgan and George Rogers Clark, and Lewis's Lts. Isaac Shelby and John Sevier.

INDIAN FORCES

The Indian army included about 425 Shawnee warriors. The Shawnee, whose name meant "the southern people," were closely related to the Kickapoo, who spoke an almost identical language. For centuries, they had lived scattered across the eastern United States. But around 1725, they had begun to settle in Ohio, where in 1774 most lived.

The Shawnee had five subgroups: the Chalawgatha (also spelled Chillicothe), the Mequashake, the Thawakila, the Kispoko, and the Peckuwe (also spelled Piqua). Each claimed certain traditional rights within the tribe. The Chalawgatha and Thawakila, for example, contended that only men from their subgroups should serve as the tribe's principal chiefs. The Kispoko made similar claims about war leaders.

This portrait by an unknown artist depicts Angus McDonald. Forty-seven in 1774, he lived at Glengarry, his estate near Winchester. (Author's collection)

About 150 Mingos fought with the Shawnees. The Mingos were a product of the Beaver Wars, when the tribes of the Iroquois confederacy had attempted to incorporate thousands of defeated enemies. Many descendants of captives, and of Caughnawagas, Catholic converts who had separated from the Mohawks, ultimately moved to Ohio, where they became known as the Mingo.

About 125 Delaware, Kickapoo, Miami, Ojibwe, Ottawa, Potawatomi, and Wyandot volunteers constituted the remainder of the army. Although the leaders of those tribes had rejected appeals to join the war against the Virginians, individual warriors answered the call. Family ties or sympathy with the Shawnee and Mingo cause prompted some. Others just wanted scalps or plunder.

Indian warriors usually fought in units of about 20, from which some were detached to hunt for the unit's food. Many who fought at Point Pleasant were descendants of traders or captives, or had themselves been captured and adopted. Private Thomas Collet of Skidmore's company found the body of his dead brother, the adopted Shawnee George Collett, on the field at Point Pleasant.

Indian commanders and warriors dressed identically. Most wore only a loincloth, leggings and moccasins. Some also wore hunting shirts like those of the Virginians. With feathers or porcupine quills rising from their hair, dangling nose rings and earrings, and faces painted in stunning designs, they appeared terrifying in battle.

Area of Ohio Indians

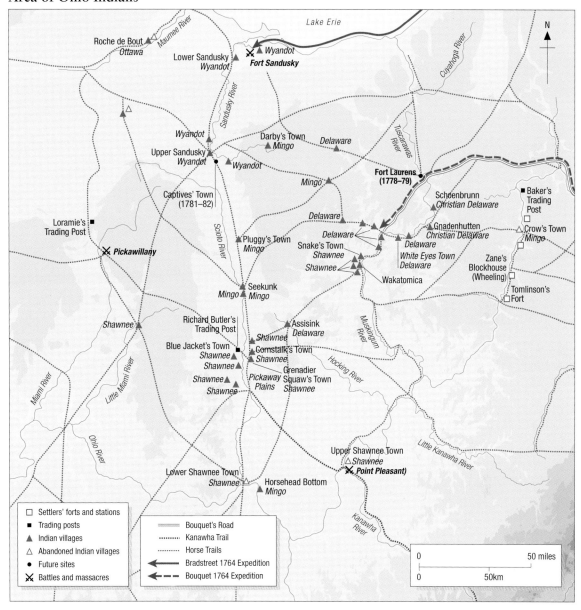

The Indians used firearms of different calibers, including smoothbore muskets; rifles; and fusils, small muskets usually used for hunting. Many carried weapons obtained in battles and raids, often the .75-cal. British Long Pattern Musket. The Virginians' rifles gave them an advantage in accuracy in exchanges of gunfire beyond about 50yd. The Indians, however, who preferred smoothbore weapons, had an offsetting advantage. They rarely fired single projectiles from their weapons. Most used rounds of one large ball, and three smaller balls of as little as .25 caliber.

Many Indians also carried bows, usually from 4 to 6ft long, and arrows tipped with scrap metal or stone. Such easily portable weapons had a range of more than 100yd, and were as accurate as smoothbore muskets. Indians

This firelock from an Indian musket, found in 2010 at the site of Grenadier Squaw's Town, is probably from a weapon used at Point Pleasant. (Author's photograph)

used them if they lacked firearms or had exhausted their supplies of powder or balls. For close combat the Indians used tomahawks, war clubs, and knives.

Although Indian women were not trained to fight in wars, Cornstalk's sister Nonhelema joined the outnumbered Indian army that fought at Point Pleasant. Described by contemporaries as several inches taller than six feet, she was called by the Virginians the Grenadier Squaw. She left behind at her village, Grenadier Squaw's Town, her 11-year-old son Tamenatha, whose father was Richard Butler.

The Indians warred with the American colonists just as they fought one another. Tribes were usually at war with other tribes. In 1774, the Miami were at war with the Cherokee, the Ojibwe with the Sioux, the Iroquois and Mingo with the Catawba, and all of the Ohio Indians with the Chickasaws of Mississippi.

Indian wars were unrestrained conflicts, in which the age or sex of enemies was disregarded, and whole tribes risked extermination. In 1730, the Fox of Wisconsin almost vanished in a war with the French and the Ohio Indians. When they tried to escape their enemies by migrating to Pennsylvania, an army of Ohio Indians trapped 800 near what is now Arrowsmith, Ill. On September 9, 1730, they killed 600 Fox men, women, and children, and captured the others.

In Indian war, prisoners became the property of the warriors who took them. Unless adopted or enslaved, adult males, and sometimes females, might be tortured to death and even ritually eaten. Children were usually adopted.

Because Indian wars were between small groups, Indian commanders sought above all to avoid casualties. Any trick or tactic that would allow enemies to be killed or captured without risk was used. They preferred raids and massacres to battles, and ambushes to engagements in which enemies could fight on even terms.

The Indians' way of war created the impression that they were treacherous and cruel. Their frequent retreats in battle also left some with the mistaken belief that they were cowardly. "They will not stand cutting like the highlanders or other British troops," wrote James Smith, "but this proceeds from a compliance with their rules of war rather than cowardice."

The Indians' behavior also appeared undisciplined. Before and after combat, they were often beyond the power of anyone to command. But in battle, Smith wrote, they were disciplined masters of the small-unit maneuvers that produced victories in battles in the western woods.

Indian boys, who had learned at an early age to survive alone in the woods, and to use the weapons they would carry in combat, began at 12 to learn such maneuvers. While living as a Mingo, Smith had watched them practice encircling areas of various sizes to surround enemies, and forming hollow squares for defense. He had seen a mile-wide line of widely dispersed warriors advance through the woods indefinitely without losing order, with each man following the lead of the warrior to his right. Such maneuvers, Smith concluded, required a subtler discipline than that known to British or colonial soldiers. "It is easier," he wrote, "to learn to move and act in concert in close order in the open plain than to act in concert in scattered order in the woods." In combat in wooded terrain, he judged, the Indians were "the best disciplined troops in the known world."

During the French and Indian War, the Indians told Smith, the ratio of colonial to Indian casualties was about 50:1. During Pontiac's War, it fell to about 10:1. In Lord Dunmore's War, Smith thought, the ratio was about 3:1.

This monument at Logan Elm State Memorial, near Circleville, Ohio, commemorates Nonhelema. (Author's photograph)

"None will suppose we had a contemptible enemy," Capt. John Stuart wrote many years later, "who has any knowledge of the exploits performed by them... They are now dwindled to insignificance ... and futurity will not easily perceive the prowess of which they were possessed."

ORDERS OF BATTLE

POINT PLEASANT, OCTOBER 10, 1774
Commander killed or mortally wounded (K)

Commander wounded (W)

Commander not present at battle (NP)

VIRGINIA (1,130) [1]
Colonel Andrew Lewis, County Lieutenant of Botetourt County, Commander

Major Thomas Posey, Quartermaster General

AUGUSTA COUNTY REGIMENT (12 COS.) (560)
Colonel Charles Lewis, County Lieutenant of Augusta County, Commander (K)

Company of Capt. George Matthews (65)

Company of Capt. Alexander McClanahan (65)

Company of Capt. George Moffat (55)

Company of Capt. John Dickinson (W) (25)

Company of Capt. Samuel McDowell (50)

Company of Capt. Benjamin Harrison (45)

Company of Capt. Andrew Lockridge (30)

Company of Capt. John Skidmore (W) (35)

Company of Capt. Samuel Wilson (K) (25)

Company of Capt. Joseph Haynes (60)

Company of Capt. John Lewis (60)

Company of Capt. William Nalle (45)

BOTETOURT COUNTY REGIMENT (11 COS.) (510) [2]
Colonel William Fleming, Colonel of the Botetourt County Regiment, Commander (W)

Major William Ingles, Quartermaster General

Pvt. John Todd, Aide-de-camp

Company of Capt. John Lewis (70)

Company of Capt. Philip Love (40)

Company of Capt. John Murray (K) (55)

Company of Capt. John Stuart (40)

Company of Capt. Robert McClanahan (K) (30)

Company of Capt. Henry Pauling (50)

Combined Company of Capt. Matthew Arbuckle and Capt. James Ward (65) [3]

    Capt. Matthew Arbuckle, Commander

    Capt. James Ward, Second in command (K)

Bedford County Company of Capt. Thomas Buford (K) (50)

Field's Culpeper and Dunmore County Companies (3 cos.) (110)

    Colonel John Field, Colonel of the Culpeper County Regiment, Commander (K)

Culpeper County Company of Capt. James Kirtley (40)

Culpeper County Company of Capt. William Chapman (35)

NOT PRESENT AT BATTLE [4]

Dunmore County Company of Capt. George Slaughter (35)

FINCASTLE COUNTY REGIMENT (8 COS.) (285) [5]

Colonel William Preston, County Lieutenant of Fincastle County, Commander (NP)

Colonel William Christian, Colonel of Fincastle County Regiment, Acting Commander

PRESENT AT BATTLE [6]

Company of Capt. William Russell (45)

Watauga Association Company of Capt. Evan Shelby (50)

NOT PRESENT AT BATTLE [7]

Company of Capt. William Robertson (35)

Company of Capt. Walter Crockett (30)

Company of Capt. William Campbell (30)

Company of Capt. William Herbert (25)

Company of Capt. John Floyd (45)

Kentucky Pioneer Company of Capt. James Harrod (25)

INDIAN (700) [8]

SHAWNEE (425)

Cornstalk, Silver Heels, Nimwha, Black Fish, Blue Jacket, Puckeshinwa, Black Snake, Captain Johnny, Black Hoof, Commanders

MINGO (150)

Pluggy, Commander

OTHER INDIANS (125)

Unknown commanders, probably including the Delaware Buckongahelas

1. Approximately 1,365 officers and men in 31 companies advanced from Camp Union. About 1,130 in 24 companies were at Point Pleasant. The numbers are estimates based on company numbers recorded on different dates.

2. The Botetourt County Regiment included four independent companies from other counties. They were a Bedford County company and three companies led by Col. John Field. Those included two Culpeper County companies and a Dunmore County company led by Field's son-in-law George Slaughter.

3. Arbuckle's company included a small company earlier led by Capt. James Ward.

4. This company arrived at the battlefield on October 14, 1774.

5. The Fincastle County Regiment included two independent companies, Shelby's Watauga Association Company and Floyd's Kentucky Pioneers.

6. These companies were detached to the Botetourt County Regiment at the time of the battle.

7. These companies arrived at the battlefield after fighting had ended.

8. The total and numbers by tribal units are estimates. The Delaware chief White Eyes told Dunmore that 700 Indians had advanced toward Point Pleasant. Fleming estimated their numbers at the battle at 700–800 and Isaac Shelby at 800–1,000.

OPPOSING PLANS

VIRGINIAN PLANS

Dunmore's objective was to compel the Ohio Indians to agree to allow Virginians to settle east and south of the Ohio River. The Virginia governor, who knew little about the Indians or warfare in the western woods, believed that his goal could be achieved by effective diplomacy supported by the threat of military action.

Dunmore modeled his campaign on a successful operation against the Ohio Indians ten years before. In 1764, Gen. John Bradstreet had led a British army across Lake Erie to Sandusky Bay. At the same time, Col. Henry Bouquet had marched with another to the forks of the Muskingum River. There, without offering battle, the Indians had agreed at a council with Bouquet to end Pontiac's War and surrender their prisoners.

The groundwork for a similar success in 1774 had already been laid. The Seneca chief Guyasuta and the great Delaware chief White Eyes had secured the agreement of all of the Ohio tribes other than the Shawnees and the Mingos. All that remained, Dunmore believed, was to advance into Ohio with a force that would overawe the isolated Shawnees and Mingos.

This Ross Straight statue in Buckhannon, W. Va., depicts the Delaware commander Buckongahelas holding his dead son Mahonegon, killed by a Virginian in 1773. (Photograph by Ross Straight)

To field such a force, Dunmore could summon the militia of Virginia's frontier counties. Those counties extended across an area more than 300 miles long. Most of their populations, moreover, were east of the western range of the Appalachians, across which there were passable routes only in the northeast and southwest. Dunmore therefore decided to recruit separate armies in the northeast and southwest, which then would unite at a site west of the mountains, on the Ohio River.

The Northern Army would form around men already west of the Appalachians, most of whom had participated in Maj. Angus McDonald's expedition against Wakatomica. They were in Wheeling; Pittsburgh; and Redstone Old Fort, now Brownsville, Pa. Additional companies, to be recruited both west and east of the mountains. They would meet at Wheeling to form the Northern Army.

Bouquet's 1,500-man army included 250 Virginia militiamen led by Andrew Lewis. Thomas Buford, John Field, Charles Lewis, and Alexander McClanahan, who would fight at Point Pleasant, were among Lewis's company commanders. This hand-colored Pierre Canot engraving, which illustrated William Smith's 1766 *Account of the Expedition Against the Ohio Indians in the Year 1764*, shows Indians returning captive children to Bouquet at what is now Coshocton, Ohio. The 278 released captives included John Gibson and Simon Girty. (Library of Congress, Prints and Photographs Division)

The Southern Army would consist of companies recruited in southwestern Virginia. It had an obvious route to an assembly point. The Kanawha Trail led directly from the Great Wagon Road to the mouth of the Kanawha River on the Ohio River. The companies forming the Southern Army would meet where the trail crossed the Greenbrier River, at a site at present-day Lewisburg, Va. that would be named Camp Union.

The Southern Army's commander, Col. Andrew Lewis, had previously led a militia army against the Ohio Indians. In February 1756, he and 263 men had marched west from Ingles Ferry to join a force of 130 Cherokees. They had then moved together down the Big Sandy River. But by the time the Virginians had reached the Ohio, they had exhausted their food and been forced to abandon the campaign.

Then the Virginians had lacked the logistical capacity for such an ambitious mission. Now they would have adequate supplies. They would consume beef, provided by cattle herded forward as they advanced, and bread, made from flour carried by packhorses or watercraft.

The flour for the Northern Army would be carried by watercraft to Wheeling, and on to the place where it would meet the Southern Army. The animals would be collected at Redstone, herded to Wheeling, and then down the eastern bank of the Ohio to the place the two armies would join. The Southern Army's flour and animals were to be carried to Camp Union by packhorses, and then to a supply base at the mouth of the Elk River, at present Charleston. A fleet of canoes built there would then carry the flour to the mouth of the Kanawha River on the Ohio, as advancing units of the army herded the cattle down the Kanawha Trail in stages.

Dunmore and Lewis initially agreed to unite the armies at the mouth of Kanawha. Effecting such a rendezvous at a distant location in the wilderness, however, would be a formidable challenge. The Virginia governor's failure to recognize either its difficulty or importance would almost lead to disaster.

Confusion would arise because the two commanders did not judge the optimal location for their rendezvous by the same criteria. Lewis assumed that the purpose of joining the armies was to enhance the power with which the Virginians could overcome opposition as they advanced to the main concentration of Shawnee villages on the Pickaway Plains. It seemed obvious to him that the armies should combine at the mouth of the Kanawha, from which the Kanawha Trail and Scioto Trail led directly toward their objective.

Dunmore, however, believed that the mere appearance of the armies would compel the Indians to request a peace council, and that the site of the council was the proper site for the armies to meet. When he was told that the council would be at the mouth of the Hocking River, Dunmore decided to have the armies meet there. When he later learned that the Shawnees and Mingos had refused to attend the council, he concluded that they would attend if his army advanced toward the Pickaway Plains. The impatient Virginia governor, unwilling to delay such an advance by the additional two to three days needed to join Lewis at the mouth of the Kanawha, instead ordered Lewis to join his army at a site near the Pickaway Plains.

Because the Indians had attacked neither Bradstreet's nor Bouquet's army in 1764, Dunmore also believed that they were unlikely to attack either his or Lewis's. He maintained that assumption even after receiving accurate intelligence that it was unfounded. Friendly Delawares, who informed him that the Mingos and Shawnees had decided on war, told him that that 700 Indians had left the Pickaway Plains to battle the Virginians.

Despite the spectacular successes of the Ohio Indians against British forces, Dunmore seems to have assumed as well that, if the Indians did attack, they would be unable to defeat either his or Lewis's army. Lewis, who lacked the information available to Dunmore, camped at Point Pleasant with no knowledge of the Indians' intentions or capacities. He and his commanders, however, also believed that the Southern Army would prevail if attacked. No Indian army had ever faced 1,100 frontier riflemen. If battle commenced, Lewis's men would scatter and find cover behind trees and logs. Then, in a contest of firearms at a distance of about 100yd, they would demonstrate their superior skill with their weapons.

INDIAN PLANS

The refusal of the other Ohio Indians to join them left the Shawnees and Mingos in a difficult position. Even with sympathetic volunteers from other tribes, they could field an army of only 700 against the 2,400 Virginians in Dunmore's and Lewis's armies. Logistical constraints, moreover, limited their ability to conduct operations. They could send raiders in small parties to distant locations. But they could not offer battle by the whole Indian army far beyond the Ohio River.

The Indian commanders, who believed that their best chance of victory lay in attacking the separate Virginia armies in sequence, decided to go into battle as soon as one reached the Ohio. In deciding which to attack first, and when to offer battle, the Indians had good sources of conventional intelligence available. Indian scouts watched the two armies advance, and examined abandoned camps to determine their sizes.

The Indian commanders also relied on a very different kind of intelligence, which was provided by Indian shamans. American prisoners reported with astonishment the degree to which the Indians relied on such information. In 1756, James Smith was with encamped Mingos and Ojibwes when a woman reported seeing armed men in the nearby woods. Before investigating, the Indians asked the Ojibwe shaman Manetohca to determine whether they were enemies. After accurately determining from a burned bone that the intruders were only wolves, "he said we might all go to sleep for there was no danger, and we accordingly did... The Indians believed what he told them on this occasion as well as it had come from an infallible oracle." In 1792, 12-year-old Oliver Spencer saw Blue Jacket ask the female Mingo shaman Coohcoocheh to foretell the fate of the Indian army that would fight at the battle of Fort St Clair on November 6, 1792. When she responded an hour later "in wild and nearly incoherent notes" that the Indians would be successful, the Indians became "as confident of victory as if the enemy already were in retreat."

On the basis of their intelligence, the Indian commanders decided to attack the Southern Army first. When Lewis's force reached the Ohio, the Northern Army was only two to three days away. The Indians then learned that Christian's advancing Fincastle County Regiment would soon join Lewis's army. They decided to attack the Southern Army's camp at Point Pleasant before either Dunmore or Christian arrived.

Experience had taught the Indians that casualties were fewest when they fought dispersed against a surrounded enemy. If an enemy attacked a segment of their encircling line, the Indians fell back, and enlarged the circle or separately surrounded the attackers. The effectiveness of such tactics against British regulars had impressed Bouquet. A commander, he wrote, "cannot discover them tho from every tree, log or bush, he receives an incessant fire... He will find himself surrounded by a circle of fire, which, like an artificial horizon, follows him everywhere."

Lewis's camp, however, which was protected by wide rivers on two sides, could not be surrounded. The Indians therefore were forced to modify their usual tactics. An Indian line from the Ohio to the Kanawha, the commanders decided, would attack the Virginians and drive them back into a small area between the rivers. There, they anticipated, the trapped Virginians would suffer heavy casualties, break through the Indian line in panic, and flee back down the Kanawha Trail.

Because of the nature of the field, the size of Lewis's army, and the compelling need to drive it back to Virginia, the Indians expected much higher casualties than they usually incurred in battle. They feared the effect of so many losses on their ability to defeat Dunmore's army in a subsequent engagement. But few doubted that they could defeat Lewis's army.

Dunmore had maps by the cartographers John Mitchell and Lewis Evans to plan his campaign 1755. This detail from Evans's map shows the area of operations. Pittsburgh was at the site marked "Ft. Du Quesne" in the upper right. Camp Union was opposite the mouth of "Howard C." on the "Green Briar R." in the lower right. The Pickaway Plains was to the right of the letter "G" above the center on the left. (Prints and Maps Division, Library of Congress)

THE CAMPAIGN AND BATTLE

FROM BAKER'S TRADING POST TO WAKATOMICA

As Connolly waited for a response to his assertion of authority in Pittsburgh, others planned western surveying expeditions in the spring. In Winchester, Fairfax's friend Angus McDonald, a major in the Frederick County militia, intended to survey land on the Ohio River. John Field, colonel of the Culpeper County militia, was to lead a surveying party down the Kanawha River. William Preston, the County Lieutenant of Fincastle County, planned to send the 23-year-old frontiersman John Floyd on a similar expedition to Kentucky.

Three other young frontiersmen planned to lead men down the Ohio River to found the first settlements in Kentucky. Alarmed by the fate of Boone's and Russell's settlers, they would go without their families to claim land and build cabins. Twenty-eight-year-old James Harrod was to guide the first party from Tomlinson's Fort. Thomas Cresap's 32-year-old son Michael was to lead another from Pittsburgh to the mouth of the Muskingum River.

The practices of the Indian shamans were ancient. Centuries before Lewis halted at his 4th Ohio Camp, these figures had been carved in a rock 4 miles to the north. They probably depict details of a famous shaman's vision at the site, now Leo Petroglyph State Memorial in Leo. (Photograph by Tom Walton)

There, at present Williamstown, W. Va., some were to settle while others followed him to Kentucky. Twenty-two-year-old George Rogers Clark was to go to the mouth of the Little Kanawha. There, at present-day Parkersburg, W, Va., settlers would arrive to form another party to go to Kentucky.

On January 24, the sheriff of Westmoreland County arrested Connolly for his actions. When Dunmore's agent promised to appear for trial in Hannastown on April 6, the sheriff released him. Connolly then fled back to Virginia.

In March, Harrod's party went down the Ohio. Cresap's party soon followed. By March 28, men in canoes were arriving daily at Clark's camp. That day, Connolly returned to Pittsburgh. Men recruited by Girty then occupied abandoned Fort Pitt, which Connolly renamed Fort Dunmore. As Connolly began establishing the new West Augusta District of Virginia, the British at last responded to the Boston Tea Party. On March 31, the government in London announced that British soldiers and ships would close the port of Boston indefinitely on June 2.

On April 6, Connolly arrived for his trial at the Hannastown tavern that would serve as the Westmoreland County courthouse. It was to be the first proceeding in the first court to open west of the Appalachians. But the assembled judges and dignitaries received a surprise. Connolly brought with him Girty and 150 men.

After threatening to arrest the judges, Dunmore's agent dispersed the Pennsylvanians. On April 8, Crawford, on behalf of the judges, and Smith, on behalf of the Westmoreland County commissioners, wrote to Governor Penn asking for immediate help. Soon, they hoped, hundreds of Bedford County militiamen would arrive to restore order.

On April 9, when Floyd and his surveyors left for Kentucky, 13 men from a hunting party arrived at Clark's camp. When they reported that Indians had killed three of their companions, the 80 settlers at the camp demanded that Clark lead them in an attack on Horsehead Bottom, an Indian village further down the Ohio.

Clark, who wanted a more experienced commander to lead the expedition, sent a messenger to Cresap, who was 15 miles upriver. "To our astonishment," Clark later wrote, "our intended general was the person who dissuaded us from the enterprise, alleging that the circumstances were suspicious but that there was no certainty of war." They all, Cresap, advised, should return to Wheeling to get more information. "The measure," Clark remembered, "was adopted. "In two hours we were underway."

When McDonald, whose party was surveying farther down the Ohio, learned of their action, he too led his men back to Pittsburgh. There Connolly was recruiting militiamen to form a force to resist the expected Pennsylvania invaders. To his dismay, he found that few frontiersmen were willing to join an army that would battle Pennsylvanians. There was, however, an enemy they would gladly fight, the Ohio Indians.

Connolly learned from McKee that a visiting Shawnee had reported that Indian warriors were talking of attacking settlers near Pittsburgh. McKee, who had heard such stories before, was unconcerned. But then, on April 16, Indians at the mouth of the Beaver River fired on three men in a canoe carrying supplies to Richard Butler's trading post, killing two. The attackers, Butler later judged, probably had been Cherokees raiding in Ohio.

By the time the survivor reached Pittsburgh, Connolly had learned that Cresap's and Clark's men were in Wheeling. On April 21, he sent a letter to Cresap. Connolly, Clark remembered, asked the men to stay in Wheeling until he could determine whether there was an Indian war. On April 26, he sent Cresap a second letter. "War," Connolly wrote, "is inevitable."

No one in Wheeling had any doubt what that meant. When the Indians decided to go to war, they did not send formal declarations to their enemies. Soon there would be deceit, as at Archibald Clendennin's house at what is now Lewisburg, Va. On June 27, 1763, an apparently friendly Shawnee, invited to eat, had soon been joined by another, and then another, until there were 18. They had then killed the men, and taken the women and children. And there would be surprise, as at Enoch Brown's schoolhouse near present Greencastle, Pa. On July 27, 1764, four Delawares had entered the classroom where Brown was teaching 15 children. After killing Brown and nine of the children, they scalped two others, and took the remaining four back to Ohio. The receipt of Cresap's letter, Clark remembered, was "the epoch of open hostilities with the Indians."

After his arrest, Connolly wrote this letter to George Washington from Pittsburgh. "I have been committed to jail," he wrote on February 1, 1774, "for denying the jurisdiction of Pennsylvania at Pittsburgh and attempting to act under a commission from Virginia." (Library of Congress, Manuscript Division)

During Pontiac's War, warriors from all of the Ohio Indian tribes had attacked the frontier settlements. The Virginians at Wheeling assumed that warriors from all would do so again. On April 27, they sighted a canoe with three Indians passing on the Ohio. After pursuing it 15 miles to the mouth of Captina Creek, they killed one of the paddlers.

Forty-two miles up the Ohio from Wheeling, there were more Indians. At the mouth of Yellow Creek, opposite Joshua Baker's trading post, the Mingo John Logan had a hunting camp. On April 28, Cresap's men began marching up the river to attack Logan's camp. But Clark, who been at the camp a month before, persuaded Cresap and the others that the Indians there were not hostile.

On July 13, 1782, British rangers and Indians led by Girty would burn Hannastown. This reconstruction of the tavern that served as the Westmoreland County Courthouse is at Historic Hanna's Town, a reconstruction of the village at the original site, near Greensburg, Pa. (Photograph by Louise Tilzey-Bates – Westmoreland Heritage)

This sketch in crayon by an anonymous artist depicts John Connolly. (Courtesy of the Filson Historical Society, Louisville, Ky.)

By then, however, news of the war had spread beyond Wheeling. On April 30, 32 settlers attacked Logan's Indians. They killed eight visiting the trading post, and another two as they fled across the river. The dead included Logan's mother, brother, sister Koonay, and Koonay's two-month-old daughter, whose father was the trader John Gibson.

On May 5, Connolly posted a proclamation in Pittsburgh that Dunmore had sent from Williamsburg on April 25. The West Augusta District, it said, was threatened by attack from both Pennsylvanians and Indians. The district's militia officers, the governor ordered, were to raise forces that would be large enough to repel any assaults by either.

When a horrified McKee learned of the massacre at Baker's trading post. he dispatched messages to the main Ohio Indian chiefs. He had acted quickly, he wrote to Johnson on May 5, "to convince those people to whom they were to be delivered of our sincerity, and that we did not coun tenance those misdemeanors." But everywhere near the Ohio River, settlers decided not to await the Indians' response. "The whole country," Crawford wrote to Washington on May 8, "is vacated as far as the Monongahela."

News of the massacre spread quickly among the Mingos, who thought that the killers had been Cresap's men. Pluggy, the leading Mingo chief, was furious. Logan, who had refused to fight in Pontiac's War, had since been a voice for peace in Indian councils. But in the French and Indian War he had been a merciless raider. Now he recruited 20 warriors to follow him in seeking revenge. Soon they left for the first of four raids, from which they would return with more than 30 scalps and many prisoners.

Dunmore's annexation of Westmoreland County had attracted little interest in the Virginia House of Burgesses, where attention was focused on the conflict with Britain. The news that the British would close the port of Boston had been followed by another infuriating report. They now had decided to transfer the area north of the Ohio River from Virginia to Quebec. The house had voted to send Washington, Patrick Henry, and another Virginian to Philadelphia, to what would be called the Continental Congress. There, on September 5, representatives from the colonies would begin considering joint action to force Britain to repeal its intolerable legislation.

This monument near Yellow Creek, Ohio, commemorates the site of John Logan's hunting camp. (Photograph by Dale Benington)

On May 13, Dunmore presented to the burgesses a report he had received from Connolly the day before. The frontier, it said, was aflame. The House of Burgesses, he urged, should fund an army of Virginia militiamen to conduct offensive operations against the Indians. The following day, the house rejected the request. Existing legislation allowed the governor to raise militia units to defend the frontier counties. That, the burgesses responded, should be adequate. On May 24, the house proclaimed June 2 a day of mourning in Virginia. On May 26, Dunmore dissolved the body.

At Pittsburgh, McKee received almost daily messages from Indian chiefs saying that their warriors were not attacking settlers. But all across the frontier, the talk was of raids and massacres. "The Delaware," wrote a man in Bedford on May 30, "say that they will not go to war, but there is no dependence in them. We expect every day to hear of their striking in some quarter... The Shawnee themselves say that they have nothing against Pennsylvania, but only Virginia; but we may depend, as soon as they strike the Virginians, they will also fall on us."

Dunmore's April 25, 1774 Proclamation. (Library of Congress, Rare Book and Special Collections Division)

Five hundred miles from Bedford, British warships and soldiers began on to enforce the closure of Boston harbor June 2. That day Logan led his raiders across the Ohio River. On June 7, Connolly reported to Dunmore that he was raising militia companies, would build a fort in Wheeling and then lead a militia army from Wheeling against Indian villages in Ohio.

As McKee's despair grew, Connolly daily became more jubilant. Croghan, after learning of the collapse of the Vandalia County project, had become a reluctant supporter of his nephew's government. Penn, who had little interest in the frontier, had rejected Crawford's and Smith's pleas for aid. Crawford, disgusted by Penn's response, had offered to raise companies for Connolly's militia army. Smith, who had been asked to lead the defense of the Pennsylvania settlers against Indian raiders, was busy recruiting Bedford County companies to patrol the woods. St Clair, for whom Connolly had issued an arrest warrant, was considering flight to Bedford County.

WHEREAS I have Reason to apprehend that the Government of Pennsylvania, in Profecution of their Claim to Pittfburg and its Dependencies, will endeavour to obftruct his Majefty's Government thereof under my Adminiftration, by illegal and unwarrantable Commitments of the Officers I have appointed for that Purpofe, and that that Settlement is in fome Danger of Annoyance from the Indians alfo, and it being neceffary to fupport the Dignity of his Majefty's Government, and protect his Subjects in the quiet and peaceable Enjoyment of their Rights; I have therefore thought proper, by and with the Confent and Advice of his Majefty's Council, by this Proclamation, in his Majefty's Name, to order and require the Officers of the Militia in that Diftrict to embody a fufficient Number of Men to repel any Infult whatever; and all his Majefty's liege Subjects within this Colony are hereby ftrictly required to be aiding and affifting therein, as they fhall anfwer the contrary at their Peril. And I do farther enjoin and require the feveral Inhabitants of the Territory aforefaid to pay his Majefty's Quitrents, and all public Dues, to fuch Officers as are or fhall be appointed to collect the fame within this Dominion, until his Majefty's Pleafure therein fhall be known.

GIVEN under my Hand, and the Seal of the Colony, at Williamfburg, this 25th Day of April, 1774, in the 14th Year of his Majefty's Reign.

DUNMORE.

GOD SAVE THE KING.

In 1774, Sgt. Isaac, and Pvts. Jacob and Josiah Prickett, of Capt. Zackwell Morgan's company, built Prickett's Fort as a refuge for Monongahela River settlers. This reproduction is at the site, now Prickett's Fort State Park near Fairmount, W. Va. (Courtesy of Prickett's Fort Memorial Foundation)

On June 10, Dunmore wrote to the lieutenants of Virginia's frontier counties, urging them to summon militia companies to defend against raids. He also recommended that the southwestern county lieutenants should send men to build a fort like Connolly's at the mouth of the Kanawha River. That same day, McKee wrote a letter appealing to Johnson. An Indian war, he said, could be avoided only if Connolly was removed. The British government, he pled, must either restore the area around Pittsburgh to Pennsylvania, or send soldiers to take control of the region for the crown while the colonies' rival claims were adjudicated.

In response to Connolly's call for volunteers, the trader John Gibson and frontiersman George Aston raised companies among the Ohio River settlers. Girty, appointed a lieutenant in Aston's unit, persuaded his 19-year-old friend Simon Kenton to enlist as a private. Francis McClure assembled another company of Monongahela settlers. But as McClure's company marched to join Connolly at Wheeling, four of Logan's raiders ambushed it about 10 miles southwest of Redstone. There, on June 11, it lost its captain at McClure's Ambush.

The chances for peace, McKee knew, were rapidly vanishing. On June 14, a Delaware visiting Pittsburgh was fired on while talking to him. Four days later, as Butler was returning to Pittsburgh with a delegation of Shawnee chiefs, McKee learned that Connolly had ordered a company of 40 militiamen to arrest them when they arrived. He diverted Butler and the Shawnees to Croghan's cabin, where they hid. But when the Shawnees left to return to Ohio, militiamen shot Cornstalk's brother Silver Heels. Badly wounded, he escaped with the aid of Butler, who told him that the attack had been by Virginians, not Pennsylvanians.

Alarmed at the prospect of a war, the Iroquois sent the Seneca chief Guyasuta to urge the Ohio tribes to remain peaceful. To McKee's relief, the widely respected Delaware chief White Eyes, protector of the Christian Delaware, joined him. But after the attack on Silver Heels, White Eyes reported, 40 Shawnees had left their villages to raid the settlements.

When Connolly realized that he could not raise in the West Augusta District a militia force large enough to invade Ohio, he turned to Dunmore for aid. The Virginia governor asked McDonald to recruit volunteers in Berkeley, Frederick, and Hampshire counties, and to lead them and Connolly's men in a punitive expedition against Wakatomica and other Shawnee villages on the Muskingum River. Dunmore also offered a commission as a Virginia militia captain to Cresap, who promised to recruit men for the expedition in Maryland.

In response to Dunmore's letter of June 10, Preston asked Boone on June 20 to go to Kentucky to recall Floyd's surveyors and Harrod's settlers. The Fincastle, Botetourt, and Augusta county lieutenants then raised militia companies to patrol the woods around their settlements. In the most likely area of Indian attack, the Kanawha, New, and Greenbrier river settlements across the western range of the Appalachians, three militia companies began searching for signs of raiders. On June 27, Indians ambushed Capt. John Dickinson's company, killing one and wounding two at Dickinson's Fight.

Field and his son Ezekiel were at Kelly's Station when Indians struck. Although they killed Kelly and captured Ezekiel, Field escaped, wearing only a shirt. Captain John Stuart, who led one of the militia companies defending the New and Greenbrier river settlements, met him fleeing on the Kanawha Trail. "His body," Stuart recalled, "was grievously lacerated with briars and brush, and worn down with fatigue and cold, having run in that condition from the Kanahway, upwards of eighty miles through the woods."

In response to McDonald's request, several famous captains, including Daniel Morgan, James Wood, John Tipton, and William Linn, raised Berkeley, Frederick, and Hampshire County companies. By July 10, they were marching west on Braddock's Road. That day Dunmore left Williamsburg for Greenway Court, Fairfax's estate near Winchester, from which he would manage the frontier war. The following day, signs of Indian raiders were found near Hannastown.

In 1778, Alexander McKee would flee Pittsburgh with Simon Girty and the trader Matthew Elliott to fight with the British during the Revolutionary War. For the next 17 years he would be the chief British agent among the Ohio Indians, and also prosper as a trader. This 1760 telescope, which belonged to McKee, is displayed at Fort Malden National Historic Site in Amhersburg, Ontario. (Photograph by Alexandra Deckerf)

As the Mingos and Shawnees raided, McKee, Guyasuta, and White Eyes worked to keep the other Ohio tribes from joining them. Even Logan, who thought Cresap's men had killed his relatives, tried to limit the scope of hostilities. After killing the settler John Roberts and his wife and children, he left a war club at their cabin. Wrapped around it was a letter, written for him by the captive William Robinson in ink made from gunpowder. "Captain Cresap – What did you kill my people on Yellow Creek for?" it began. "I have been three times to war since; but the Indians are not angry, only myself. Captain John Logan. July 21, 1774," the letter ended.

Soon the area around Ebenezer Zane's blockhouse in Wheeling was crowded. Connolly arrived to build his fort, which he would name Fort Fincastle. McDonald appeared with his men, and then Cresap and Clark, with an oversized company. When Crawford arrived with his men, the expedition against Wakatomica would begin.

About 400 men would advance by canoes down the Ohio to the mouth of Captina Creek. They then would follow the Captina Trail and the Muskingum Trail to Wakatomica, Snake's Town, and three smaller Shawnee villages on the Muskingum River. They would have no packhorses, and would have only the food they could carry with them to eat. But they could leave food with the canoes. If they could advance and return in long enough daily marches, they would find supplies waiting for them before the food they carried was exhausted.

At Greenway Court, Dunmore learned that a hundred Shawnee warriors in eight war parties were now raiding the settlements. The expansion of the war, he concluded, presented an opportunity. He would, he decided, lead an army much larger than McDonald's into Ohio himself. With it, he would demonstrate to the Indians and Pennsylvanians alike Virginia's dominion over

Greenway Court was about 4 miles southeast of Winchester. Fairfax's land office still stands at the site. (Courtesy Preservation Virginia)

the frontier. He would force the Mingos and Shawnees to sue for peace and return prisoners at a council like Bouquet's ten years before. On July 24, he issued a flurry of orders. Adam Stephen, the Berkeley County Lieutenant, was to raise a regiment and march to Greenway Court. The Frederick and Hampshire county lieutenants were to dispatch with him additional companies beyond those already with McDonald. Preston and the Augusta and Botetourt county lieutenants were to raise regiments and march to the mouth of the Kanawha River.

On July 25, Crawford arrived with his recruits, who would remain in Wheeling to finish Fort Fincastle, while McDonald's men attacked Wakatomica. On July 26, canoes carried the Virginians to the mouth of Captina Creek. After reaching the Muskingum River, they marched upstream. To avoid detection, they then left the Muskingum Trail and moved up the east side of the river.

But on August 2 they saw Indians, and discovered along their route a prepared ambush site. Late that afternoon, they entered a swampy area 6 miles south of Wakatomica. Marching in three columns, the Virginians found that only a single, narrow path led through the swamp to high ground beyond. When the first Virginians emerged from the path and began climbing up toward the high ground, about 40 Indians attacked. For a half-hour, the Virginians struggled forward through the swamp under fire, and then moved right and left to form a line beyond it. When there finally were enough, Cresap led them forward and drove the Shawnees from the field. Two Virginians were killed. Linn and Pvt. John Hardin, who would become a famous Kentucky militia leader, were among the five wounded.

Leading the Virginians who had crossed the swamp, Cresap pursued the fleeing Indians up the Muskingum to opposite the Shawnee towns. McDonald and the rest of the army arrived to join them at camps across the river from Wakatomica and Snake's Town. That night, Indian emissaries appeared, saying that the Shawnees wanted peace and would return two women taken during raids. As they talked, the Indians at the villages fled with their prisoners, leaving behind only a few warriors.

Cresap, who expected a Shawnee attack the following morning, decided to move first. Two hours before dawn on August 3, his men crossed the Muskingum River and entered Wakatomica. There a warrior died and a Virginian was wounded before the last Indians fled. Finding the other villages empty, the Virginians burned them and the surrounding cornfields.

Their food, however, was now almost exhausted. With their remaining supply, and a cow and some almost inedible corn found at the villages, the Virginians started back to the Ohio River. "The men," Thomas remembered, "became exceedingly famished on this march, and I myself, being so young, was so weak that I could no longer carry anything on my person." At last, the starving men reached the river, feasted on the food left in the canoes, and returned upriver to Wheeling.

Many Indians preferred war clubs to tomahawks as weapons in close combat. The clubs often had wooden spikes or were studded with pieces of metal. (Jeff Dearth Collection)

Northern Army Area of Operations

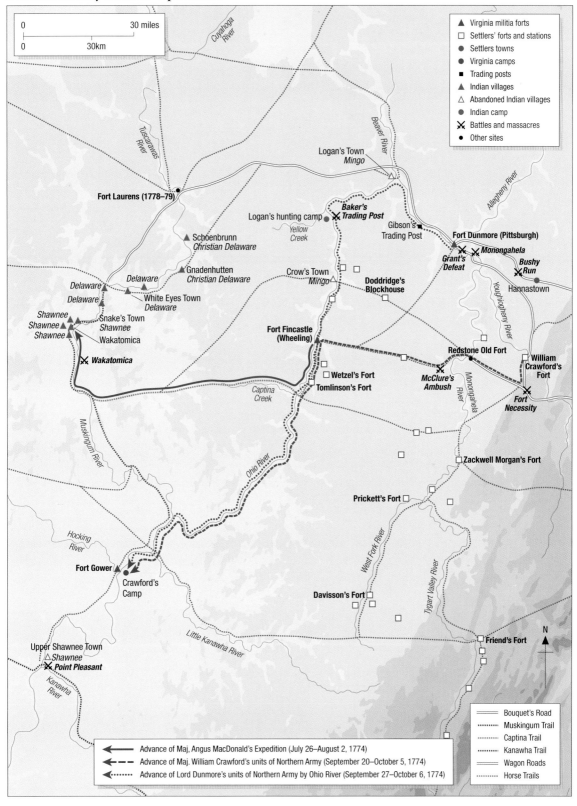

0   30 miles
0   30km

Virginia militia forts
Settlers' forts and stations
Settlers towns
Virginia camps
Trading posts
Indian villages
Abandoned Indian villages
Indian camp
Battles and massacres
Other sites

Cuyahoga River
Tuscarawas River
Beaver River
Allegheny River

Logan's Town
Mingo

Fort Laurens (1778–79)

Logan's hunting camp   **Baker's Trading Post**
Yellow Creek   Gibson's Trading Post
Schoenbrunn   **Fort Dunmore (Pittsburgh)**
Christian Delaware   **Monongahela**
Grant's Defeat   **Bushy Run**
Gnadenhutten   Crow's Town   **Doddridge's Blockhouse**   Hannastown
Christian Delaware   *Mingo*
Delaware   Youghiogheny River
Delaware   White Eyes Town
Delaware   *Delaware*
Shawnee   Snake's Town
Shawnee   *Shawnee*
Shawnee   Wakatomica   **Fort Fincastle (Wheeling)**
Wakatomica   Redstone Old Fort   **William Crawford's Fort**
Wetzel's Fort   **McClure's Ambush**
Tomlinson's Fort   **Fort Necessity**
Captina Creek   Monongahela River

Ohio River

Zackwell Morgan's Fort

Prickett's Fort   West Fork River

Hocking River

Fort Gower   Tygart Valley River
Crawford's Camp

Davisson's Fort

Little Kanawha River

Upper Shawnee Town   **Friend's Fort**
△*Shawnee*
Point Pleasant   N

Kanawha River

Advance of Maj, Angus MacDonald's Expedition (July 26–August 2, 1774)
Advance of Maj. William Crawford's units of Northern Army (September 20–October 5, 1774)
Advance of Lord Dunmore's units of Northern Army by Ohio River (September 27–October 6, 1774)

Bouquet's Road
Muskingum Trail
Captina Trail
Kanawha Trail
Wagon Roads
Horse Trails

Connolly named the fort in Wheeling after another of Dunmore's titles, Viscount Fincastle. In 1776, when Virginia's new state legislature would elect Patrick Henry the state's first governor, Fort Fincastle would be renamed Fort Henry. During the Revolutionary War, it would be attacked by Indians and British rangers on September 1, 1777, and be besieged from September 11 to 13, 1782. This marker in downtown Wheeling is at the site. (Photograph by Rick Robol)

FROM WAKATOMICA TO POINT PLEASANT

When McDonald returned to Wheeling, he found new orders from Dunmore. He was to join the Virginia governor at Greenway Court, where men were gathering for Dunmore's campaign. The men he had led to Wakatomica were to march to Redstone, where the packhorses and cattle for the campaign would be collected. The other militiamen were to remain in Wheeling or Pittsburgh. Crawford was to recruit more men.

As McDonald rode east, other commanders were meeting 250 miles to the south. In 1732, John Lewis and his family had left Ireland to become the first settlers in the upper Shenandoah Valley. The town of Staunton had grown up around his fort, Fort Lewis. In 1756, his son Andrew had built another Fort Lewis, in present Salem, Va. Now the County Lieutenant of Botetourt County, Col. Andrew Lewis would command Dunmore's Southern Army.

Two men soon joined Lewis. William Fleming, the colonel of Lewis's Botetourt County Regiment, arrived from Belmont, his home in what would later become Roanoke. Next came Lewis's younger brother Col. Charles Lewis. In 1750 he had built his own stronghold, which was known as Fort Lewis Plantation. He was now the County Lieutenant of Augusta County.

On August 12, the Lewis brothers and Fleming reached Preston's Smithfield Plantation, where they met with Preston and William Christian, colonel of the Fincastle County Regiment. Dunmore, Preston announced, had ordered him to assume command of the frontier defenses. In his place, Christian would lead the Fincastle County Regiment. Charles Lewis's Augusta County Regiment, Fleming's Botetourt County Regiment, and Christian's regiment would assemble at a site on the Greenbrier River to be called Camp Union. From there, Andrew Lewis would lead the regiments to the mouth of the Kanawha River, where they would join Dunmore.

The following day, Dunmore learned at Greenway Court how far east the Indians could raid. The attack on Wakatomica, he wrote to the Earl of Dartmouth, the British Secretary of State for the Colonies, "has not yet called home those that were on this side of the mountains, for whilst I was at dinner yesterday I was informed that they were murdering a family about fourteen miles from me."

The appearance today of the high ground from which the Shawnees attacked at the battle of Wakatomica, as seen from the position of the Virginians in the swamp. The sign refers to a nearby archery range. (Author's photograph)

Dunmore's Northern Army would have about 1,200 men in three components. Stephen was bringing to Greenway Court his 500-man Berkeley County Regiment, and another 100 Frederick County men. They and the men McDonald had led to Wakatomica would form the 500-man Frederick County Regiment, which Crawford, now promoted to major, would lead. Connolly, also promoted to major, would lead approximately another 200 men waiting west of the Appalachians, who would form as West Augusta District Battalion. McDonald would serve on Dunmore's staff.

On August 27, Stephen's regiment began advancing up Braddock's Road toward Pittsburgh. A few days later, Dunmore followed with McDonald and the additional Frederick County men. When they reached Burd's Road, the Frederick County companies marched to Redstone. Dunmore and McDonald, who continued toward Pittsburgh, then stopped at Crawford's fort. Crawford, Dunmore said, was to lead the Frederick County Regiment and the army's packhorses and cattle from Redstone to Wheeling. There, after descending the Ohio from Pittsburgh, the other units of the Northern Army would join him.

In the south, Lewis's army began to take shape. There would be no trouble recruiting enough Augusta County companies. In less populous Botetourt and Fincastle Counties, however, men were reluctant to leave their families unprotected. After returning from warning Harrod and Floyd in Kentucky, Boone had raised a company, and offered to serve as the army's guide. But his men wanted to limit their service to guarding against raiders.

Russell and Floyd, however, had raised companies for the Botetourt and Fincastle County Regiments, and volunteers from other counties had come forward to swell the regiments' ranks. For the Botetourt County Regiment, Field, who had recovered from his escape from Kelly's Station, would bring two Culpeper County companies, and another from neighboring Dunmore County, which his son-in-law George Slaughter had recruited. Captain Thomas Buford would bring a Bedford County company. For the Fincastle Regiment, Harrod and his men, angry at having to abandon their new cabins at what would become Harrodsburg, Ky., had formed a company of "Kentucky Pioneers." Captain Evan Shelby would bring a company of Watauga Association men.

By August 29, most of the Southern Army companies had arrived at Camp Union, where they awaited their commander, the Fincastle County Regiment, and Slaughter's company. On September 1, Andrew Lewis arrived to lead them. That day, 600 miles to the northwest, British Gen. Thomas Gage sent soldiers to seize militia arsenals in Charlestown and Cambridge, Mass.

As Lewis waited for Christian's Fincastle County Regiment, Indians hovered around Camp Union. On September 2, they wounded a man, and on September 3 another. On September 5, they stole several horses. That day, Washington, Christian's brother-in-law Patrick Henry, and other delegates from the colonies convened in Philadelphia in the first session of the Continental Congress.

When Christian's regiment arrived on September 6, Charles Lewis led his men forward on the Kanawha Trail toward the Ohio River, 140 miles ahead. With them went more than 100 cattle, and 500 of the Southern Army's 800 packhorses, carrying 54,000lb of flour. They were to halt at the mouth of the Elk River, establish a fortified supply camp, and await the rest of the army. On September 10, Field and his Culpeper companies followed.

On September 12, Andrew Lewis and Fleming led forward the Botetourt County Regiment, augmented by Russell's and Shelby's Fincastle Regiment companies, with another 18,000lb of flour. At the same time, Dunmore reached Pittsburgh. There Stephen's regiment and Connolly's West Augusta District Battalion were ready to embark on a fleet of watercraft that would carry the army and its supplies down the Ohio.

White Eyes and the Delaware chief Captain Pipe were also there. They would go, they told Dunmore, to the Pickaway Plains to try to persuade the Mingos and Shawnees to attend a peace council at the mouth of the Hocking River. The Virginia governor, who had planned to lead the Northern Army to the mouth of the Kanawha, now announced that it would go to the mouth of the Hocking instead. He would arrive for the council, he told the Delaware chiefs, in early October.

Halting at their 2nd through 9th W. Va. Camps, Lewis's men moved slowly through the difficult country to the east of the New River. On September 20, when Crawford left his fort for Redstone, they reached their 10th W. Va. Camp. The following day, after passing the ruins of Kelly's Station at what is now Cedar Grove, they halted at their 11th W. Va. camp opposite the mouth of Cabin Creek.

On September 22, Lewis's men arrived at the mouth of the Elk River, in present Charleston. There, 108 miles from Camp Union, they joined Charles Lewis's and Field's men at their 12th W. Va. Camp, the army's supply base. The combined regiments then began building 27 large canoes to carry supplies down the Kanawha.

On September 27, Christian's Fincastle County Regiment and Slaughter's company marched from Camp Union. On the same day, Dunmore left Pittsburgh with Stephen, Connolly, their men, and the army's flour and other supplies. As the flotilla moved down the Ohio at about 3 miles an hour, the Virginia governor's guides pointed out the sights on the river's banks. Nineteen miles downstream on the left was the trading post of Capt. John Gibson and his brother George. Ten miles farther on the right was John Logan's village, abandoned the year before. Twenty-three miles downstream on the left was Baker's trading post, and on the right the site of Logan's hunting camp. Twenty-one miles farther on the right was the site of Crow's Town, a Mingo village abandoned in 1772.

On September 30, Lewis left a small guard and 50 cattle at his 12th W. Va. Camp, and advanced to his nearby 13th W. Va. Camp, from which the canoes would descend the Kanawha. On the same day, Dunmore's flotilla, and Crawford's men, cattle, and packhorses reached Wheeling.

There Crawford received new orders. He and his Frederick County Regiment were to drive the cattle 60 miles down the

Michael Cresap lived in this house, which he completed in 1764. It is now a museum in Oldtown, Md. (Courtesy of the Irvin Allen/Michael Cresap Museum)

Southern Army Area of Operations

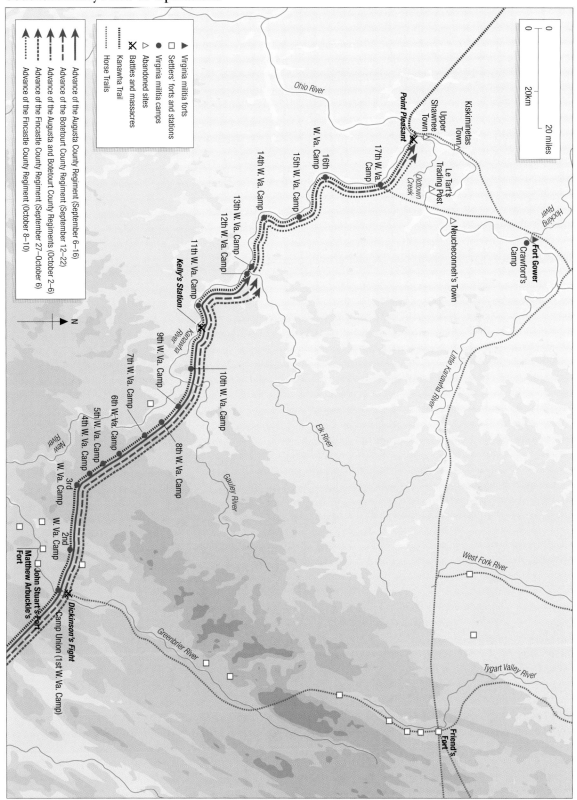

Legend:

▶ Virginia militia forts
□ Settlers' forts and stations
● Virginia militia camps
△ Abandoned sites
✖ Battles and massacres
⋯ Kanawha Trail
⋯ Horse Trails

Advance of the Augusta County Regiment (September 6–16)
Advance of the Botetourt County Regiment (September 12–22)
Advance of the Augusta and Botetourt County Regiments (October 2–6)
Advance of the Fincastle County Regiment (September 27–October 6)
Advance of the Fincastle County Regiment (October 8–10)

N

Map labels: Ohio River, Point Pleasant, Upper Shawnee Town, Kiskiminetas Town, Le Tart's Trading Post, Oldtown Creek, Neucheconneh's Town, Crawford's Camp, Fort Gower, Hocking River, Little Kanawha River, 17th W. Va. Camp, 16th W. Va. Camp, 15th W. Va. Camp, 14th W. Va. Camp, 13th W. Va. Camp, 12th W. Va. Camp, 11th W. Va. Camp, Kelly's Station, Kanawha River, 9th W. Va. Camp, 10th W. Va. Camp, 8th W. Va. Camp, 7th W. Va. Camp, 6th W. Va. Camp, 5th W. Va. Camp, 4th W. Va. Camp, 3rd W. Va. Camp, 2nd W. Va. Camp, New River, Elk River, Gauley River, West Fork River, Matthew Arbuckle's Fort, John Stuart's Fort, Dickinson's Fight, Camp Union (1st W. Va. Camp), Greenbrier River, Tygart Valley River, Friend's Fort

eastern bank of the Ohio and camp opposite the mouth of the Hocking River. It was a site Crawford knew well. On October 27 and November 7, 1770, he and Washington had camped there while surveying. Now he was to build at the mouth of the Hoching a supply base that would be named Fort Gower.

The men who arrived in Wheeling brought with them alarming rumors about what was happening east of the Appalachians. American militiamen in Massachusetts, it had been reported, were battling Gage's British soldiers. All shared a hope that Dunmore's campaign would end at the peace council on the Hocking. A quick peace with the Indians, Crawford's brother Valentine wrote to Washington from Wheeling on October 1, would allow the men there "to assist you in relieving the poor distressed Bostonians – if the report here is true that General Gage has bombarded the city of Boston."

When White Eyes and Captain Pipe reached the Pickaway Plains, they found an Indian army of about 700 assembled. To their disappointment, the Mingos and Shawnees rejected their peace council proposal. After the Delawares left, Cornstalk, the Shawnee war leader, then addressed his warriors. The next day, he announced, they would march to attack Lewis's army.

From a small wigwam, a shaman removed what looked like part of an old blanket that had been wrapped and tied. From the object, one of the five war bundles of the Shawnee subgroups, he removed a series of sacred items. To Cornstalk, he gave an ancient tomahawk, and to four other commanders clusters of hawk feathers to attach to their hair. He then removed a small wooden figure. A carved Shawnee warrior with a bow and arrows, it would preside over the war dance.

To the beat of drums. the Indians sang war songs and danced for hours around a war post, attacking it with tomahawks to display their frenzy. Cornstalk, who had argued for sending emissaries to Dunmore's peace council, joined the others. But the worried Shawnee commander had little enthusiasm for the battle to come. It would not be enough, he knew, to send Lewis's men fleeing back to Virginia. Even an overwhelming victory would be disastrous if it left his army too weakened then to defeat Dunmore's.

After sleeping for a few hours, the excited warriors began forming the single-file column in which they would advance. The shaman tied the bundle to a long pole to form the war *beson*, the standard under which the Shawnees would fight. Then, before dawn, the Indian army began moving down the Scioto Trail.

Delayed by a day of torrential downpour, Lewis's men left their 13th W. Va. Camp on October 2. As they and their supply canoes went down the Kanawha, halting at their 14th through 17th W. Va. Camps, Dunmore's men were moving down the Ohio. Seventeen miles from Wheeling, they reached Captina Creek on

In 1774, William Preston built this house at Smithfield Plantation, now a historic site in Blacksburg, Va. (Courtesy of Historic Smithfield Plantation)

This photograph of the New River Gorge National River, taken about 5 miles west of Lewis's 4th W. Va. Camp, shows the formidable terrain through which the Southern Army advanced. (National Park Service photograph)

the right and, after another 69 miles, the mouth of the Muskingum. Thirteen miles on they reached the mouth of the Little Kanawha on the left. The Hocking was 12 miles ahead. The mouth of the Kanawha, Dunmore's scouts informed him, was about 50 miles by land beyond the Hocking, and by the twisting Ohio River about 80.

Lewis's army, Dunmore thought, probably had by now reached the mouth of the Kanawha. The Virginia governor wrote a letter to Lewis, ordering him to proceed immediately to the new rendezvous site. Girty, his young friend Simon Kenton, and another scout then sped down the river by canoe ahead of Dunmore's fleet. But when they reached the Kanawha, they found that Lewis was not there. Girty then carved a message in the trunk of a hollow tree, saying that Dunmore's letter to Lewis was concealed inside.

On October 6, as Christian's advancing regiment halted at Lewis's 12th W. Va. Camp on the Elk River, Dunmore's flotilla reached its destination. He found Crawford waiting and his captains, including Clark, who now had his own company. They had begun building Fort Gower. But there were no Indians.

A few hours later, Girty and Kenton arrived. When they reported that Lewis was not at the mouth of the Kanawha, the frustrated Virginia commander asked Girty to go back down the river and up the trail toward Camp Union to find Lewis's army. As Dunmore prepared another letter to Lewis, Stephen quickly wrote one to the Southern Army commanders as well. After a rest, Girty went downstream again.

That same day, Lewis's army reached the Ohio. From their 18th W. Va. Camp, the view was stunning. "The dense forest clothed in its autumnal tints," Fleming wrote in his journal, "and the rivers at low water, with the Ohio resembling a lake and the Great Kanawha an estuary, the whole landscape presenting an enchanting scene. An army of weary men appreciated it and bestowed on it the name of Camp Point Pleasant."

Lewis's men soon found Dunmore's letter. But, to the Southern Army commander's annoyance, it ordered him to move his army up the Ohio to the Hocking. Lewis immediately dispatched two scouts to tell Dunmore that he had most of his army at the mouth of the Kanawha, but was awaiting the remainder and could not move immediately to the Hocking because his packhorses were exhausted.

On October 7, White Eyes and Captain Pipe arrived at the mouth of the Hocking. There would be no council, they told the Virginia commander.

Ohio Area of Operations

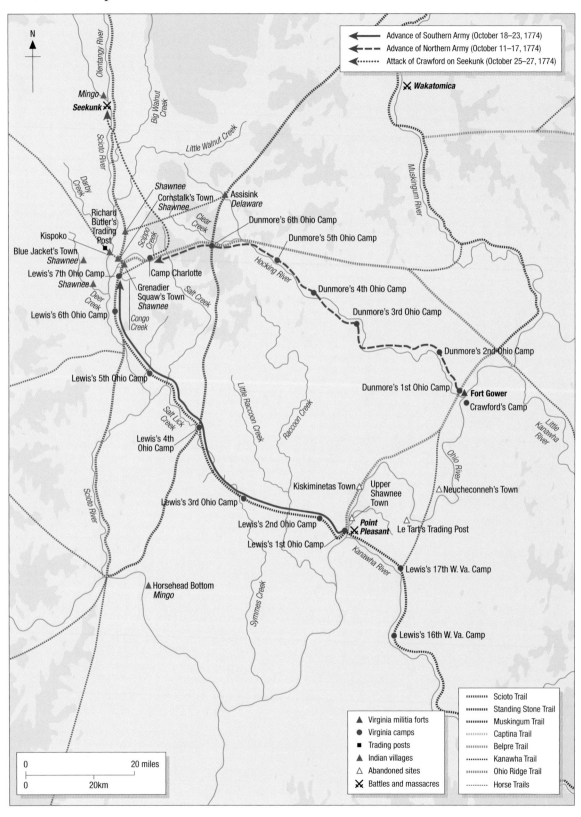

N

Legend:
- Advance of Southern Army (October 18–23, 1774)
- Advance of Northern Army (October 11–17, 1774)
- Attack of Crawford on Seekunk (October 25–27, 1774)

Wakatomica

Mingo
Seekunk

Olentangy River
Big Walnut Creek
Little Walnut Creek
Muskingum River
Scioto River
Darby Creek

Shawnee
Cornstalk's Town
Shawnee
Assisink
Delaware
Dunmore's 6th Ohio Camp
Dunmore's 5th Ohio Camp

Richard Butler's Trading Post
Kispoko
Blue Jacket's Town
Shawnee
Lewis's 7th Ohio Camp
Shawnee
Camp Charlotte
Clear Creek
Scippo Creek
Hocking River
Dunmore's 4th Ohio Camp
Dunmore's 3rd Ohio Camp

Grenadier Squaw's Town
Shawnee
Salt Creek
Deer Creek
Lewis's 6th Ohio Camp
Congo Creek

Dunmore's 2nd Ohio Camp
Dunmore's 1st Ohio Camp
Fort Gower
Crawford's Camp
Little Kanawha River

Lewis's 5th Ohio Camp
Salt Lick Creek
Little Raccoon Creek
Raccoon Creek
Ohio River

Lewis's 4th Ohio Camp

Scioto River

Lewis's 3rd Ohio Camp
Kiskiminetas Town
Upper Shawnee Town
Neucheconneh's Town

Lewis's 2nd Ohio Camp
Point Pleasant
Le Tart's Trading Post
Lewis's 1st Ohio Camp
Kanawha River

Lewis's 17th W. Va. Camp

Horsehead Bottom
Mingo

Symmes Creek

Lewis's 16th W. Va. Camp

Map symbols:
- ▲ Virginia militia forts
- ● Virginia camps
- ■ Trading posts
- ▲ Indian villages
- △ Abandoned sites
- ✕ Battles and massacres

Trails:
- Scioto Trail
- Standing Stone Trail
- Muskingum Trail
- Captina Trail
- Belpre Trail
- Kanawha Trail
- Ohio Ridge Trail
- Horse Trails

0   20 miles
0   20km

The Mingos and Shawnees were set on war. His army, the angry Dunmore decided, would go forward to the Pickaway Plains.

On October 8, Christian advanced from the 12th W. Va. Camp. Leaving Slaughter's company to guard the army's supply base, his other companies marched with 350 cattle toward the mouth of the Kanawha. The canoes that accompanied them carried another 27,000lb of flour downstream.

As the Fincastle men moved down the Kanawha, scouts were scurrying between Dunmore's and Lewis's camps in two-day journeys and five-day round trips. On October 8, Lewis's scouts found Dunmore's army at the Hocking. On the same day, Girty delivered Dunmore's and Stephen's letters to Lewis. Fleming, to whom Lewis showed Stephen's letter, wrote in his journal that night, "Col. Stephen in his to Col. Lewis says he hears disagreeable news from Boston but cannot assert it."

Girty then returned to the Hocking with letters from Lewis to Dunmore, and Fleming to Stephen. Dunmore's army, Lewis urged, should join his at the mouth of the Kanawha. Lewis's men, Fleming wrote to Stephen, were reluctant to leave a site where they blocked Indian raiders from using the Kanawha Trail and were closer to the Shawnee villages than Dunmore's army. If Lewis's men were ordered to move, he added, "I am convinced it would be attended by considerable desertions."

As the tireless Girty paddled back up the Ohio on October 9, three more scouts sent by Dunmore, including the famous frontiersman William McCulloch, arrived at Point Pleasant with another letter to Lewis. The Northern Army, Dunmore informed Lewis, would march directly toward the Pickaway Plains on October 13. Lewis's army was to meet his at noon on October 18 at a ridge southeast of the Pickaway Plains.

Consternation spread as Lewis told his officers the news. After experiencing the difficulty of rendezvousing at even a prominent site in the wilderness, Dunmore had now chosen a vague location about 50 miles away, in the heart of where the hostile Indians were concentrated. "What calculations he might have made for delay or other disappointments that might happen to two armies under so long and difficult a march through a trackless wilderness," Capt. John Stuart of the Botetourt County Regiment would write, "I could never guess."

Dunmore's decision would also leave the Southern Army exposed alone to an Indian attack. That prospect, however, did not alarm Lewis and his officers. "Encamped in the forks of the river, in safe possession of a fine encampment," remembered Major Thomas Ingles, "we thought ourselves a terror to all the Indian tribes on the Ohio."

At noon on October 9, the Virginians assembled for their usual Sunday religious service. As the afternoon passed, and McCulloch waited to carry Lewis's response back to Dunmore, he met Stuart. He thought, he told the Southern Army captain, that the Indians would probably attack Lewis's army soon.

As McCulloch and the other scouts began paddling back to the mouth of the Hocking, hundreds of Indians were moving north on the wooded

Indian tomahawks were used both in close combat and as throwing weapons at distances up to about 15yd. This tomahawk with a modern handle, unearthed in 2010 at the site of Grenadier Squaw's Town, was probably used at Point Pleasant. (Jeff Dearth Collection)

ridge across the Ohio River from Lewis's camp. About 3 miles upriver from the mouth of the Kanawha, they halted, built 74 rafts, and waited. At 6.25pm, the last sunlight left the sky. At 9.12pm, the last moonlight. Then, concealed by darkness, the first rafts silently began to cross the river.

THE BATTLE OF POINT PLEASANT

At 5.30am on October 10, sunrise was still an hour away at the Indians' camp. Their commander was on familiar ground. When Cornstalk had been a boy, the trading post of James Le Tart, the first British trader in the Ohio Country, had been 11 miles to the east, near the Shawnees in Neucheconneh's Town and Kiskiminetas Town. In 1738, raiding by the Catawbas had forced Le Tart and the Shawnees to leave. In 1751, the Shawnees had built the village the British called Upper Shawnee Town at the mouth of Oldtown Creek. But in 1756, when Lewis's Virginians had advanced up the Big Sandy, they had withdrawn again, to villages on the Scioto River.

The Shawnees' preparations for battle were completed. They had slept for a few hours as they always did while campaigning, leaning against trees or logs or poles extending between forked sticks, their weapons at hand, ready to awaken instantly to respond to an attack. They had eaten as they always ate before a battle. Twelve deer had been killed, and the venison cut into the exact number of pieces the army had warriors. Then the pieces had been roasted and their condition studied by the shaman. Now, after burying their tools, kettles, and superfluous clothing, they were ready to meet the enemy.

At last, like a great, uncoiling snake, a three-quarter-mile-long column of Indians began moving in single file towards Oldtown Creek and the Virginians' camp. It was late, thought the Indians' worried commander. They would advance slowly in the darkness. And when the first sunlight appeared in a half-hour, Virginia scouts might discover them before they reached their battle positions.

Beyond Oldtown Creek, the Indians would advance on a low ridge above the Ohio. About 200–300yd to its left, a parallel ridge overlooked Crooked Creek. Beyond the ridges, the column would descend to the low ground through which Crooked Creek flowed. Its head would reach the creek's mouth on the Kanawha River, almost half a mile from the Ohio. The column then would become the line from river to river in which the Indians would attack the Virginians.

They would fight, the Shawnee commander knew, on a field defined by three main features. Along two, the Kanawha and Ohio rivers, the Virginians' tents extended in lines. The third was a massive ridge east of Crooked Creek. Its 250ft-high walls, in places almost vertical, formed a two-mile-long arrowhead aimed directly toward the point where the rivers met, about a half-mile away.

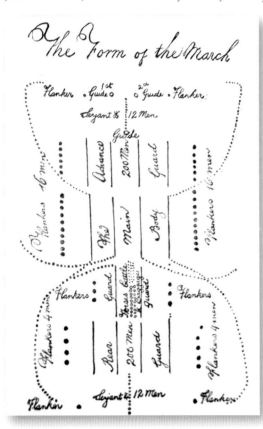

William Fleming's drawing of the order of march from Lewis's 13th W. Va. Camp to Point Pleasant, with the Augusta County Regiment as the left column and his Botetourt County Regiment the right. (Author's collection)

As the Indians moved silently through the dark woods, the tired pickets at Lewis's camp were awaiting relief from Capt. Alexander McClanahan's company, which would provide the new day's sentinels. The half-mile-long line they guarded, behind which hundreds of cattle and horses were sleeping or grazing, was the long side of a triangle. On the two shorter sides, each more than 500yd long, tents stretched along the rivers. Those on the Kanawha were for 560 men in the 12 companies of Charles Lewis's Augusta County Regiment. Those on the Ohio were for 570 in Fleming's Botetourt County Regiment, which included seven Botetourt County companies, Field's two Culpeper County companies, Buford's Bedford County company, and Russell's and Shelby's detached Fincastle Regiment companies.

The Ohio River today, as seen from the area where Fleming's Botetourt County Regiment camped. (Photograph by Ed Lowe)

Along the Ohio there were a few fires. Tired of their diet of beef and bread, some of the men had risen early to hunt for deer and turkey. Joseph Hughey and James Mooney of Russell's company, who served as scouts for the army, went first. Sergeant James Robertson of Shelby's company and Sgt. Valentine Sevier of Russell's followed. Soon the hunters moved past the pickets on a 250yd-wide area of ground that extended north from the camp toward the ridge on which the Indians were advancing. About 40ft above the Ohio, which was 75yd to its left, it rose about 20ft higher than the low ground to the right, through which Crooked Creek flowed below the high ridge.

As the Indians were advancing, Lewis was at this location, overlooking the Kanawha River (left) and Ohio River (right), in a senior officer's tent like that used by these re-enactors. (Photograph by Ed Lowe)

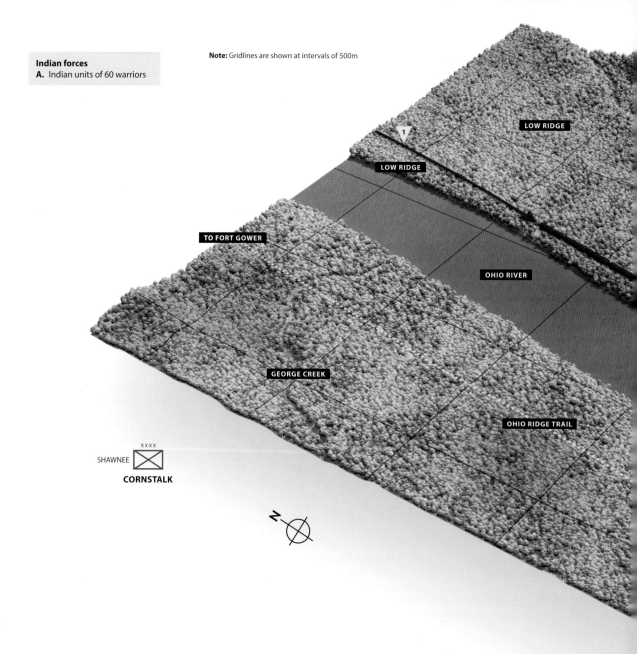

Indian forces
A. Indian units of 60 warriors

Note: Gridlines are shown at intervals of 500m

LOW RIDGE

LOW RIDGE

TO FORT GOWER

OHIO RIVER

GEORGE CREEK

OHIO RIDGE TRAIL

SHAWNEE XXXX

CORNSTALK

N

▼ EVENTS

1. Indians advance toward the mouth of Crooked Creek.

2. Colonel William Fleming's Botetourt County Regiment column advances toward Indians.

3. Colonel Charles Lewis's Augusta County Regiment column advances toward Indians.

4. When the Indians learn of the advancing Virginia columns, the warriors at the head of the Indian column take positions to ambush the Virginians.

5. Indians attack the Augusta County Regiment column and force the Virginians back.

6. Indians attack the Botetourt County Regiment column and force the Virginians back.

7. Unit of Indians advances down bed of Crooked Creek toward its mouth.

8. The remainder of the warriors in the Indian column join in the attack.

9. The ¾-strength companies of Capts. Shelby, Russell, Love, and Buford reinforce the Botetourt County Regiment column.

10. The ¾-strength companies of Capts. Dickinson, Harrison, Skidmore, and Wilson reinforce the Augusta County Regiment column.

THE INDIAN ATTACK: OCTOBER 10, 1774, 6.45AM–7.30AM

Having advanced through the darkness, the Indian forces approach the Virginian positions.

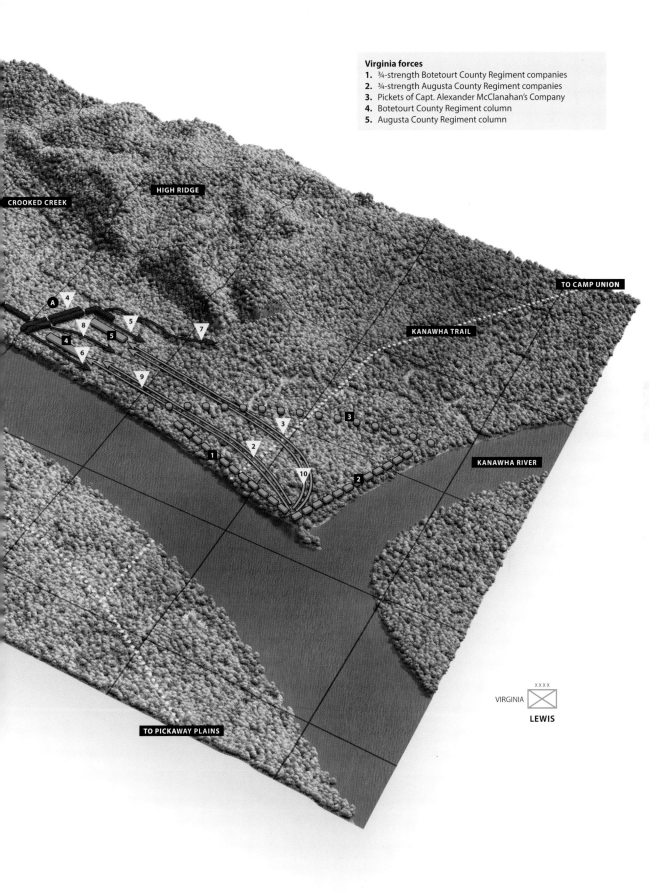

Virginia forces
1. ¾-strength Botetourt County Regiment companies
2. ¾-strength Augusta County Regiment companies
3. Pickets of Capt. Alexander McClanahan's Company
4. Botetourt County Regiment column
5. Augusta County Regiment column

CROOKED CREEK

HIGH RIDGE

TO CAMP UNION

KANAWHA TRAIL

KANAWHA RIVER

TO PICKAWAY PLAINS

VIRGINIA

XXXX

LEWIS

57

This portrait by an unknown artist depicts James Robertson. Five years after the battle, he would build Fort Nashborough, which would become Nashville. (Courtesy of the Tennessee State Museum)

6.00–9.00am

When Hughey and Mooney had gone north about a mile and a half, the first, dim light of morning revealed Indians ahead in large numbers. It also disclosed the two Virginians to the adopted Shawnee Tavenor Ross. After fighting with the Virginians at Wakatomica, he had decided to return to the Indians. A ball from his musket killed Hughey.

As Cornstalk, alarmed that the Indians had been seen, cautiously led his column forward, Mooney raced back to the Virginians' camp. He reached the northernmost of the Botetourt County officers' tents, which belonged to Capt. John Stuart. "I discovered a number of men collected around him as I lay in bed," Stuart remembered. "I jumped up and approached him, to know what was the alarm, when I heard him declare he saw above five acres of land covered with Indians, as thick as one could stand beside another." Robertson and Sevier then arrived to confirm the presence of Indians.

When Stuart informed the Virginia commander, Lewis lit his pipe. After a few moments' pause, he ordered his drummers to beat "To Arms," the signal for the Virginians to assemble for battle. He then decided to send about a quarter of his army up the Ohio in a reconnaissance in strength.

Fleming and Charles Lewis would go north with Botetourt and Augusta County Regiment columns. Each of the regiments' four most senior captains would go with them, leading 100 men. To avoid delay, Lewis had his company captains choose among their just awakened men 12 or 13 from each unit who were ready to go. Soon the selected men were arriving at their assembly point near the confluence of the rivers. Shelby, Russell, Buford, and Capt. Philip Love, who would accompany Fleming in the column on the left, placed the arriving Botetourt Regiment men in their column's two files. Charles Lewis's captains, John Dickinson, Benjamin Harrison, Samuel Wilson, and John Skidmore, whose column would advance on the right, did the same for the Augusta Regiment men.

The 150yd-long columns then went forward toward the place where Mooney had seen the Indians. Mooney led Fleming's column on a route about 100yd to the right of the Ohio River. Another scout led Charles Lewis's column on a parallel course about 150yd to the right of Fleming's.

By 6.33am, when the sun at last rose over the high ridge beyond Crooked Creek, the head of the Indian column was nearing the creek. Scouts then reported that the Virginia columns were approaching from the Indian column's right. The news confirmed Cornstalk's fear. Discovered before they had formed their line from the Kanawha to the Ohio, the Indians would have to begin the battle here. After summoning forward more men from the column, he positioned his warriors ahead of the Virginians in cover to ambush them.

Fleming's column advanced about 550yd beyond the northernmost pickets guarding the Botetourt County Regiment tents. Charles Lewis's trailed about 100yd behind. Then, recalled an officer who had remained in the camp, "Three guns went off, which was immediately followed by several hundreds."

The first musket balls killed Lewis's scout. Hundreds more then hit the advancing Augusta County column. As the Virginians paused in shock, the Indians reloaded, and fired a second volley. Before they fired a third, Lewis's men had scattered behind large trees and logs. When the Indians ahead of Fleming's column heard the shots, they immediately opened fire. Musket balls killed Mooney. Fleming's men then scattered too.

When attacked from the front, the Virginians in each file were to wheel forward, away from the other file, to form a line at the front of the column. As the officers tried to move the men into lines, and to join the left flank of Lewis's line to the right of Fleming's, they attracted Indian fire wherever they could be seen.

Lewis soon fell. He was shot, Christian was told, "in clear ground as he had not taken a tree. He turned, handed his gun to a man and walked to camp, telling the men as he passed along, 'I am wounded, but you go on and be brave.'"

Fleming fell too. Two balls hit his left arm. Then another struck his chest. But the wounded Botetourt County colonel urged his men not to retreat. "With great coolness and deliberation," an eyewitness remembered, "he stepped slowly back and told them not to mind him but to go up and fight."

As the Augusta and Botetourt column captains tried to form their lines, they faced a difficult challenge. The men they tried to move into positions, drawn from different companies, refused to obey their commands. "There was no one officer who had his own men," Floyd wrote after the battle, "and it was impossible for the officers to collect their own men so that when they saw any doing no good, and ordered them to advance, they refused and said they would be commanded by their own officers."

Under the heavy fire, moreover, the number of captains began to dwindle. In the Augusta column, Wilson soon fell dead, and Dickinson and Skidmore wounded. In the Botetourt column, Buford was mortally wounded.

On the left, Evan Shelby, Russell, and Love maintained a degree of order. There the Ohio River provided a point upon which the Virginians could anchor their left flank. Falling back toward the end of their column, the Botetourt Regiment men were able to begin forming a rough line from their left toward the Augusta County men to their right.

This scene of autumn woods near Wellston, Ohio, shows the conditions in which the Virginians and Indians fought. During the battle, the Indians concealed beneath piles of leaves bodies that would later be carried from the field. "I saw a young man," Capt. John Stuart recalled, "draw out three that were covered with leaves beside a large log in the midst of the battle." (Author's photograph)

Charles Lewis carried these surgical tools at the battle; they are displayed at the Mansion House Museum in Point Pleasant. (Photograph by Ed Lowe)

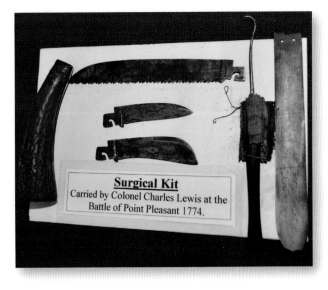

Surgical Kit
Carried by Colonel Charles Lewis at the Battle of Point Pleasant 1774.

THE INDIAN ATTACK, OCTOBER 10, 1774, 6.45AM (PP. 60–61)

A column of 700 Indians advancing toward the Kanawha River discovered that two parallel columns of 150 Virginians were approaching, marching in the opposite direction. The Indians then halted their advance and prepared to ambush their enemies. The scene shows Shawnee warriors commencing their attack on the Virginia column on the Indian left, which contained Augusta County militiamen led by Col. Charles Lewis. A Shawnee shaman (1) has earrings hanging from ear lobes that were partially severed and distended, a common practice among Ohio Indians of the time, and wears the roach headdress usually worn by Shawnee warriors in ceremonies. He is holding the tribe's battle standard (2), the *beson*, a pole carrying one of the Shawnee subgroups' sacred war bundles. The Shawnee war chief Cornstalk (3), who has given the command to fire, is waving a tomahawk (4)

taken from the war bundle, probably one of the first axes with a metal blade obtained by the Shawnees from the French in the 17th century. This Shawnee warrior (5) has begun the battle by firing his musket. Ahead, one of two scouts (6) leading Lewis's Virginians has been hit by a musket ball. Behind the scouts, partially concealed by the trees and undergrowth, Lewis's 150 Virginians (7) are advancing in a two-file column. This warrior (8), who lacks a musket, is firing an arrow from his bow. Concealed by the foliage, warriors (9) extending back through the woods along the length of the column now fire into the Virginians. Beyond the scene, 150yd to the right, Indians hearing the fire have begun to attack Col. William Fleming's parallel Virginia column of Botetourt County militiamen.

On the right, where only Harrison remained among the captains, there was chaos. Charles Lewis's column had ceased to be an organized militia force. What followed, however, showed the capacity of even a leaderless collection of experienced frontiersmen in a battle in the woods. The Virginians, Stuart judged, "had no knowledge of the use of discipline or military order." But they also "were well skilled in their own manner of warfare." Some of the men Charles Lewis had led raced back to the camp seeking safety. But most found places behind trees and logs, searched for targets, and fell back only when pressed too hard.

The appearance today of the area where the head of Charles Lewis's column was attacked, near Pioneer Cemetery. (Author's photograph)

The ambush had killed many Virginians. But its disruption of Cornstalk's battle plan soon became apparent. Some of the warriors at the head of his column moved forward in the bed of Crooked Creek toward its mouth. But most who had attacked the Virginians pressed their assault. As the Indians remaining in the column reached the field, they searched for positions in which they could join in the attack.

When men fleeing from the ambush reached his camp, the Virginia commander learned that the engagement was not just a skirmish. In addition to McClanahan's 65-man camp guard, he had about 750 men available to deploy, in companies reduced to three-quarter strength by the diversion of men to the columns. "Col. Lewis," Fleming wrote his wife three days later, "who, as we did not expect a general engagement, was in camp, behaved with the greatest conduct and prudence, and by timely and opportunely supporting the lines ... prevented the enemy's attempts to break into the camp."

Lewis first ordered the lieutenants of the captains who had marched with Fleming and Charles Lewis to take their companies forward to support their beleaguered commanders. Lieutenant Isaac Shelby, the lieutenants of Russell's, Love's, and Buford's companies, and about 140 men went up the route the Botetourt captains had followed. The reinforcements soon reached Evan Shelby, who had assumed command of the Botetourt men. Their arrival ended the threat of a further Indian advance. Shelby then began to extend the Virginians' position to the right, incorporating into his ranks men who had been in Charles Lewis's column.

Four Augusta County lieutenants led their men up the path that Dickinson, Harrison, Wilson, and Skidmore had followed. They entered an area where the Indian warriors were forcing back the outnumbered Virginians. But their 95 additional rifles slowed the Indians' advance.

The Virginia commander next ordered Capt. John Lewis, whose cousin of the same name led an Augusta County company, to deploy his 55-man Botetourt company in a screening line between the camp and the area where fighting raged. Behind them, he ordered the approximately 470 men of the remaining companies to begin felling trees. They were to be used to build breastworks along a line between the furthermost tents on the Kanawha and Ohio.

Charles Lewis left a pregnant widow, who named her son after his father. In 1800, the younger Charles Lewis settled near the site of the battle. The photograph shows his house about 2 miles north of Point Pleasant, which survives as Old Town Farm. (Photograph by Ed Lowe)

As the Indians continued to advance on the Virginians' right, the wounded Fleming returned to the camp. He met Charles Lewis, who already had been carried there. "I have sent one of the enemy to eternity before me," Lewis told Fleming before expiring.

When the Virginia commander learned that Fleming and Charles Lewis had fallen, he dispatched Field to take command of the units battling the Indians. With him, Lewis sent additional reinforcements. Up the route of Charles Lewis's column, Field led forward about 200 men in his two Culpeper County companies, and the Augusta County companies of Capts. George Matthews, Samuel McDowell, Andrew Lockridge, and John Lewis.

Although Shelby's reinforced Botetourt County Regiment companies had halted the Indians' advance, the Virginians on the right now had been pushed back more than 400yd from the point where they had been attacked. Field's force stopped any further Indian advance. But then Field fell. At the time, Christian was told, he was "behind a great tree, looking for an Indian who was talking to amuse him whilst some others were above him on his right hand among some logs, who shot him dead."

Worried that the Indians might advance to the mouth of Crooked Creek, and attack the camp from the east, Lewis sent about 120 men of the last remaining Augusta County companies, led by Capts. William Nalle, Joseph Haynes, and George Moffat, to stop them. After fighting in and around the bed of Crooked Creek, the Virginians reached the base of the high ridge. The Indians, recalled Stephen Mitchell, a settler who had joined Lewis's army after escaping Indian captors, then "were driven, with the loss of half their force, back upon the main body." An anonymous officer, probably Moffat, led the last company to arrive at the ridge. "I was ordered out with fifty men," he wrote, "to a certain place to prevent the Indians getting round our camp. I, with my men, run about half a mile and came to some of our men by a hill. The Indians had retreated."

The Indians forced the Augusta County companies back to this area. (Author's photograph)

Lewis had retained as a last reserve the Botetourt County companies of Stuart and Capts. Matthew Arbuckle, Henry Pauling, Robert McClanahan, and John Murray. When he learned that Field had fallen, Lewis decided to commit them. With orders that Evan Shelby was to assume command of the Virginians fighting the Indians at the front, the Botetourt captains and their almost 200 men went forward on the route that Fleming had followed.

With the new reinforcements, Evan Shelby moved to the southeast. There he forced the Indians back and began incorporating the Augusta County men into a coherent line. By 9 o'clock, he had accomplished his assignment. The Virginians on the right, recalled Isaac Shelby, finally were "in a line with the troops left in action on the banks of the Ohio by Col. Fleming." "Our people at last formed a line," Christian wrote to Preston after the battle. "So did the enemy."

9.00am to 1.00pm

The engagement had not proceeded as the Indian commanders had planned. It now threatened to become what Cornstalk had wanted to avoid, a battle of attrition. When conditions changed, and the Indians no longer had any advantage on a battlefield, Indian commanders usually withdrew their men to fight another day. But the desperate Shawnees and Mingos were uncertain that there would be another day.

The base of the high ridge in the area where the Virginians established the right end of their line. (Photograph by Ed Lowe)

The battlefield, which stretched about 600yd from the Ohio River to the high ridge, would not allow the Indians to use their usual tactics. They could not attack the Virginians' left flank, which was guarded by the Ohio. Nor their right, which rested on the high ridge. Even where the ridge's cliffs weren't vertical, the incline was so steep that a flanking movement was impractical.

Their enemies, moreover, now were beginning to recover ground. When attacked, Indian warriors usually fell back to minimize casualties, intending then to surround attackers who had advanced too far. But this battle could no longer be won by tactics designed to minimize casualties. To prevail, the Indians would have to break through the Virginia line. The Indian warriors, their commanders ordered, must not retreat. They must attack.

The stiff resistance of the reinforced Virginians had diminished the distance between the combatants. Now the tenacity of the Indians reduced it further. The Virginians could hear the Indians' shouts and taunts. Stuart heard a Shawnee chief yelling commands to his warriors. "One of my company," he remembered, "who had once been a prisoner, told me what he was saying, 'Be Strong. Be strong.'" Some of

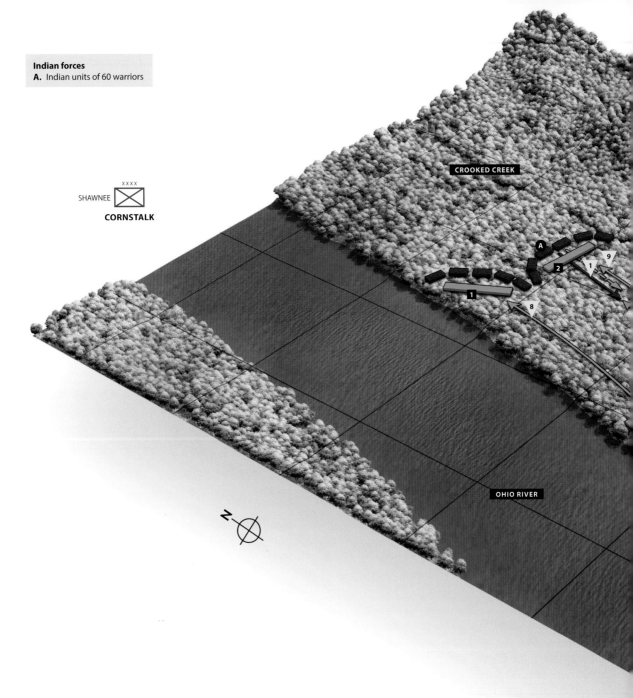

Indian forces
A. Indian units of 60 warriors

SHAWNEE xxxx
CORNSTALK

CROOKED CREEK

OHIO RIVER

EVENTS

1. Indians drive the reinforced remnant of the Augusta County Regiment column back.

2. Indians advance down the bed of Crooked Creek.

3. Captain John Lewis's ¾-strength Botetourt County Company advances to create screening line ahead of the Virginians' camp.

4. Led by Col. John Field, the ¾-strength Kirtley and Chapman Culpeper County companies, and Matthews, McDowell, Lockridge, and Lewis Augusta County companies, reinforce the Augusta County Regiment units battling the Indians.

5. The Augusta County Regiment companies of Nalle, Haynes, and Moffat stop Indians from advancing down Crooked Creek.

6. Indians retreat up Crooked Creek.

7. Nalle, Haynes, and Moffat companies secure the Virginia right flank.

8. The Botetourt County companies of Stuart, Arbuckle, Pauling, Robert McClanahan, and Murray reinforce the Shelby, Russell, Love, and Buford companies and remnant of the Botetourt County Regiment column.

9. Captain Evan Shelby establishes the Virginia line from the Ohio River to the high ridge.

THE VIRGINIA DEFENSE: OCTOBER 10, 1774, 7.30–9.00AM

The Virginians rush men forward to hold the line in the face of renewed Indian assaults.

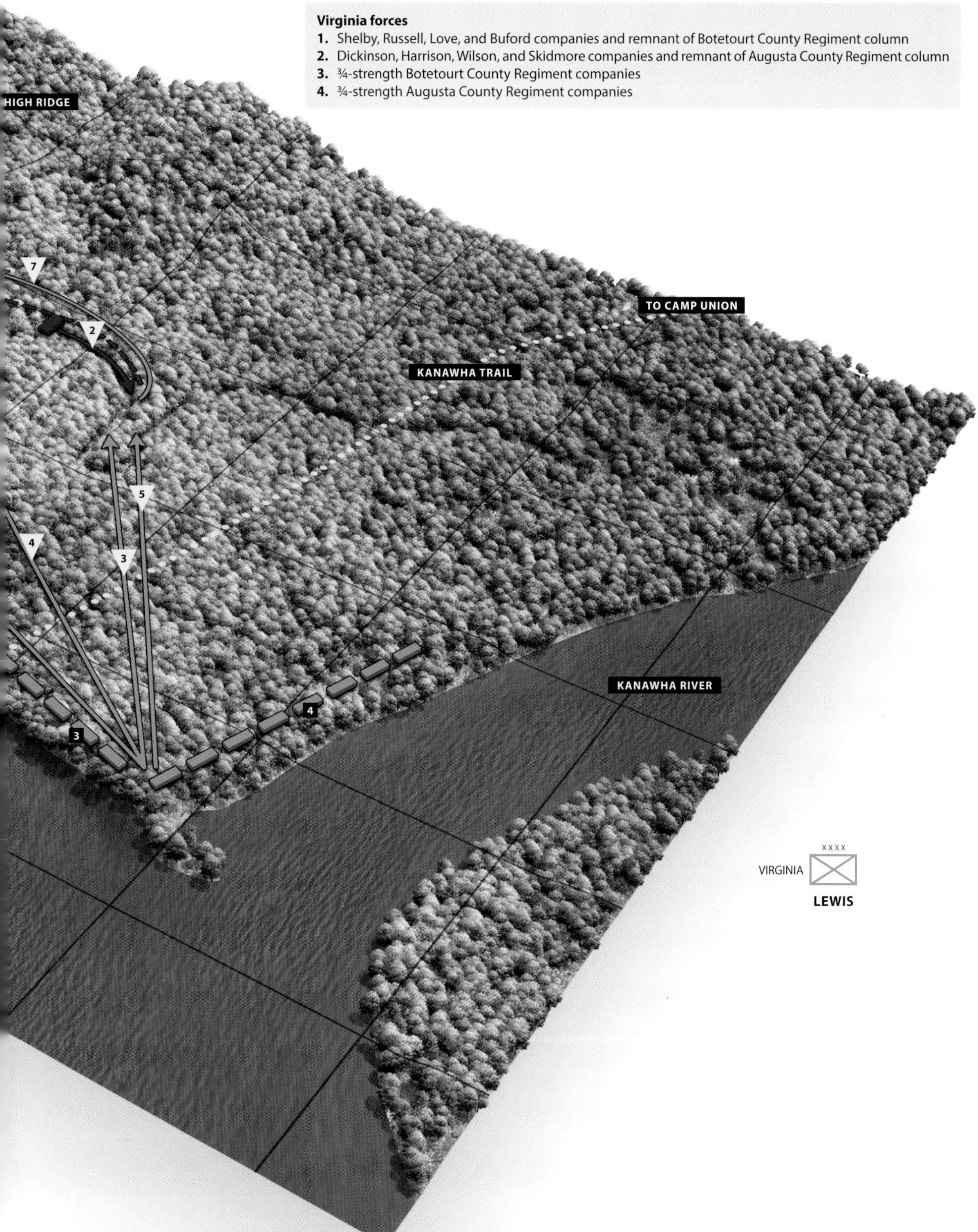

Virginia forces
1. Shelby, Russell, Love, and Buford companies and remnant of Botetourt County Regiment column
2. Dickinson, Harrison, Wilson, and Skidmore companies and remnant of Augusta County Regiment column
3. ¾-strength Botetourt County Regiment companies
4. ¾-strength Augusta County Regiment companies

HIGH RIDGE

TO CAMP UNION

KANAWHA TRAIL

KANAWHA RIVER

VIRGINIA

XXXX

LEWIS

Note: Gridlines are shown at intervals of 250m

the Indians' insults were in English. From behind trees and logs came cries of "sons of bitches" and "white dogs."

Used to fighting almost invisible warriors, the Virginians now battled an enemy they had never fought before. "The Indians," remembered Major William Ingles, "disputed the ground ... inch by inch." They showed "the greatest obstinacy, often running up to the very muzzles of our guns." "Never," wrote Fleming to a friend after the battle, "did Indians stick closer to it, nor behave bolder." "I cannot," Christian wrote to Preston, "describe the bravery of the enemy in battle. It exceeded every man's expectations."

Much of the combat, a survivor remembered, was at very close distance. The Virginians and Indians, said one, were "never above twenty yards apart, often within six, and sometimes close together, tomahawking one another." "Hide where I would," Mitchell recalled, "the muzzle of some rifle was gaping in my face and the wild, distorted countenance of a savage was rushing towards me with uplifted tomahawk."

The Virginia casualties grew steadily. Soon, in Robert McClanahan's company, the captain and lieutenant died and the ensign was wounded. In Murray's, the captain was killed, and in Arbuckle's, Capt. James Ward. Many of the militiamen suffered multiple wounds. Private John McKinney of Moffat's company returned to the Virginia camp with a musket ball wound in his left thigh, another in his left wrist, and a grievous tomahawk wound in his upper back.

Decades later, Mitchell remembered with a shudder what the combat had been like. In a series of dark dramas, individual militiamen and warriors had fought for the prize of life. "The contest," he wrote, "resembled more a circus of gladiators than a battle."

Sometimes speed and dexterity determined the outcome of the combatants' grim duels. Men who had fired their weapons raced their opponents to reload. Both knew that, at such close distance, the winner's ball would not miss.

Others were tests of judgment. Men who realized that they could not win their reloading races had to decide instantly whether to dash for cover, or towards their opponents. Those who sprinted forward, leaping over logs and fallen branches, had to weigh the chances that, if they threw their tomahawks or knives, they would hit their targets or arrive unarmed.

Sometimes men won their duels by deceit. Private Richard Burk of Russell's company, pretending that he'd been hit by a musket ball, thrashed on the ground in death throes. Too eager to claim Burk's scalp, the Indian who had fired the shot ran forward. He learned too late that Burk was alive with a loaded rifle. After taking the Indian's scalp, the satisfied Virginian took a break from the combat to eat. "I believe," he said to a companion, "I've earned my dinner."

Others, like Mitchell, survived by strength and ruthless ferocity. As he reloaded his rifle, an Indian racing forward threw a tomahawk. The Virginian dodged the weapon, which buried its blade in a tree. In vicious hand-to-hand combat, the two then wrestled for survival. Mitchell, after crippling his opponent. finally retrieved the tomahawk and killed him. The Virginian, however, had had enough. "I immediately rose," Mitchell wrote 53 years later, "and gaining a secure position behind a tree, remained there till the close of the fight, and made a thousand resolutions, if I survived this engagement, never to be caught in such a scrape again."

Here Indian Hectors fell, and there Virginian Goliaths. But the Indians had no advantage in such contests. Any ground they gained against Shelby's men was soon lost. At last, the Indians ceased their reckless attacks and began to fall back.

The line Shelby had created was rough. "There were never," wrote Capt. John Floyd, "more than three or four hundred of our men in action at once, but the trees and logs the whole way from the camp to where the line of battle was formed served as shelters for those who could not be prevailed on to advance to where the fire was." And, he added without naming names, "Many of the officers fought with a great deal of courage and behaved like heroes, while others lurked behind and could by no means be induced to advance to the front."

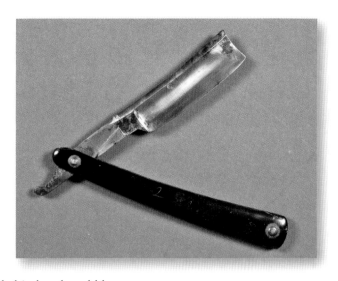

While camped at Point Pleasant, Evan Shelby shaved with this razor. After his death in 1777, it passed to Isaac Shelby, who carried it with him during the Revolutionary War. (Kentucky Historical Society, Mrs Susanna Preston Shelby Collection, 1952.44)

But the number of Virginians on the front was enough. They now, moreover, could fight the battle they had expected. On a field only 600yd wide, hundreds of eyes searched the woods for the locations of Indian muskets. A fired musket's flame and smoke attracted the attention of a dozen Virginia marksmen, each capable of targeting any Indian head, hand or foot that became visible. Protected by their covering fire, other Virginians ran or crawled forward toward the area where the musket had flashed.

Yard by yard, the Indians fell back before the Virginians' deadly rifle balls. "We pursued them," wrote Moffat, "from tree to tree." "The close underwood, and many steep banks and logs," Isaac Shelby remembered, "greatly favored their retreat."

Hour after hour it continued, with the opposing battle lines slowly but steadily moving north. And every hour the lines grew longer, as the Virginians on the left pushed forward faster than those on the right. By noon, Fleming's aide John Todd remembered, the Indians opposing the Botetourt Regiment companies had been compelled "to retreat about a mile."

But the Indians' "long retreat," remembered Isaac Shelby, "gave them a most advantageous spot of ground." At the north end of the field two long, low ridges pointed at the Virginians like prongs of a fork. The Indians falling back from the Botetourt County Regiment at last occupied the ridge upon which they had advanced that morning. The Botetourt County men then fought their way up, and occupied ground far along the ridge's length. "This advantageous post being gained about one o'clock," Todd remembered, "all the efforts of the enemy to regain it proved useless."

The Virginians on the right, however, had more difficulty. When the Augusta County Regiment companies pushed the Indians back to the other low ridge, they found refuge behind a natural breastwork of fallen tree trunks and branches. "They placed themselves behind logs," Moffat remembered, "fired on us, killed three men near me, and wounded ten or twelve more." The Augusta County men nonetheless "pushed up farther."

But after fighting for six hours, and suffering heavy casualties, Lewis's militiamen were exhausted. "Our men," Christian wrote to Preston, "could have forced them away precipitously, but not without great loss, and so

THE CLOSE COMBAT, OCTOBER 10, 1774, 10.00AM (PP. 70–71)

After hours of fighting, the Virginians have finally formed a line and begun to push the Indians back. The Indians, desperate to drive the Virginians from the field, have redoubled their efforts to break through the Virginia line. Much of the fighting now is at a close range. A Virginia militiaman **(1)** who has reloaded his rifle faster than a Shawnee warrior ahead of him is now aiming his weapon to kill the Indian. Realizing that he has lost the race to reload, the warrior **(2)** is dashing to find cover behind a tree.

Another warrior **(3)**, concealed from the Virginian by a tree, is creeping forward to attack him as another Virginian **(4)** arrives at the scene. A Virginian wounded by a thrown tomahawk **(5)** is lying on the ground. A friend **(6)** who has run to save him is battling the Shawnee who had thrown the tomahawk **(7)**. Another Virginian **(8)** is reloading his rifle as a warrior **(9)** runs forward to attack him.

concluded to maintain their ground all along it, which they did until sundown." "It appeared to the officers," remembered Isaac Shelby, "so difficult to dislodge them that it was thought advisable to stand as the line was then formed, which was about a mile and a quarter in length." "The whole line from the Ohio to us," recalled Moffat, halted "at the same time. This happened about one o'clock."

The appearance today of the low ridge held by the Indians against the Augusta County Regiment, as seen from the base of the ridge occupied by the Botetourt County Regiment. The trees in the background are on the high ridge. (Author's photograph)

1.00–11.45pm

The battle, the shocked Indian commanders knew, had been lost. Even the almost superhuman efforts of their warriors had not been enough. But the consequences of failing to drive Lewis's army back to Virginia were too dire for them to accept. Again and again, warriors tried to expel the Botetourt County Regiment from the low ridge near the Ohio. "Tho they would summon all the force they could raise," Todd recalled, "and make many pushes to break the line, the advantage of the place and the steadiness of the men defied their most furious essays." Then, Floyd wrote, "The Indians retired to a thick place where there had been a town and damned the white men for sons of bitches."

As the afternoon began to wane, the Indian attacks grew less frequent. But Lewis remained wary. Up the Kanawha, he knew, Christian's companies were advancing toward the battlefield. At 3.00pm, he dispatched messengers to the Fincastle County Regiment commander, ordering him to hasten to the field as quickly as possible.

Then it began to rain. As the leaves covering the ground grew ever wetter, the last hopes of the Indians slipped away. Many of their best commanders and warriors were dead or wounded. Even the shaman who had carried the *beson* had fallen, and the war bundle's sacred objects had been lost. All thoughts of victory abandoned, the Indian commanders decided to leave the field.

They assigned units to hold the Indian line while most of the army retired. Ordered to create the appearance that the Indians were still fighting, the remaining warriors fired, screamed, and taunted. As they performed their martial charade, other warriors fashioned litters from fallen tree branches to carry the dead and wounded. Still others raced back to the Indian camp to retrieve their buried goods and the rafts on which they had crossed the Ohio.

The stratagem deceived the Virginians. Worried that the Indians might renew their attack that night or the next day, Lewis decided to try to force them to leave the field. The high ridge beyond Crooked Creek towered above the low ridge where the Augusta Regiment companies had halted. From there, the Virginians could fire down on the Indians, and threaten to attack them from behind.

Lewis recalled from the line 150 men in Shelby's company, now led by Lt. Isaac Shelby; Stuart's company; and the company of Capt. George Mathews. At a point about 300yd behind the far right of the Augusta County Regiment

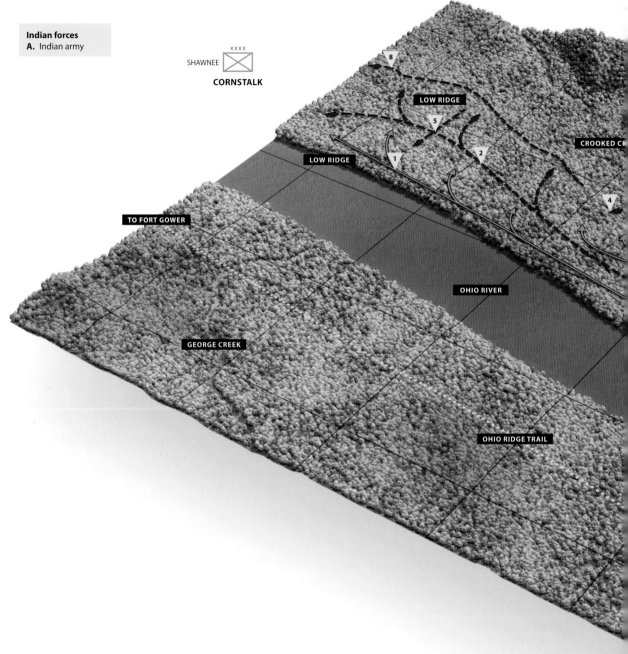

Indian forces
A. Indian army

SHAWNEE xxxx
CORNSTALK

LOW RIDGE

LOW RIDGE

CROOKED C

TO FORT GOWER

OHIO RIVER

GEORGE CREEK

OHIO RIDGE TRAIL

▼ EVENTS

1. The Botetourt County Regiment drives the Indians a mile farther, and occupies the low ridge overlooking the Ohio River.

2. The Indians retreat north and east to the low ridge overlooking Crooked Creek.

3. The Augusta County Regiment drives the Indians back to the low ridge overlooking Crooked Creek.

4. The retreating Indians, after hastily building breastworks of fallen tree trunks and branches on the low ridge overlooking Crooked Creek, halt the Augusta County Regiment advance.

5. The Indians repeatedly try to expel the Botetourt County Regiment from the low ridge overlooking the Ohio River.

6. After being recalled to the Virginia camp, the Shelby and Stuart Botetourt County Regiment companies and Matthews Augusta County Regiment Company move below the bank of the Kanawha River, up the bend of Crooked Creek, and then up a ravine to the top of the high ridge.

7. The Shelby, Stuart, and Matthews companies advance to a point overlooking the Indians and fire down on them.

8. The Indians withdraw from the field.

THE VIRGINIA COUNTERATTACK: OCTOBER 10, 1774, 11.00AM–6.00PM

Having regained the initiative, the Virginians push the Indian line backwards.

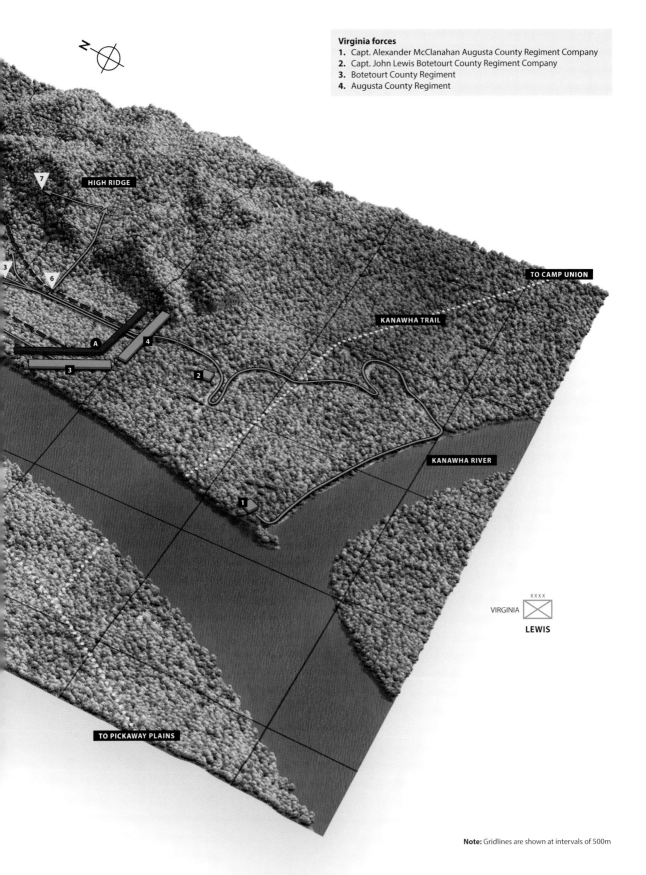

Virginia forces
1. Capt. Alexander McClanahan Augusta County Regiment Company
2. Capt. John Lewis Botetourt County Regiment Company
3. Botetourt County Regiment
4. Augusta County Regiment

HIGH RIDGE

TO CAMP UNION

KANAWHA TRAIL

KANAWHA RIVER

TO PICKAWAY PLAINS

VIRGINIA

LEWIS

Note: Gridlines are shown at intervals of 500m

75

THE HIGH RIDGE, OCTOBER 10, 1774, 5.00PM (PP. 76–77)

The advance of the Augusta County Regiment has halted at a low ridge beyond Crooked Creek, which the Indians are defending behind a crude breastwork of fallen tree trunks and branches. Three companies, led by Capts. John Stuart and George Matthews, and Lt. Isaac Shelby, have been sent to climb a much higher ridge from which they can fire down on the Indians. The scene shows the Virginians reaching the top of the high ridge. A Virginian **(1)** from Stuart's company is using a tree trunk to pull himself up the steep incline while another **(2)** has paused to catch his breath. Stuart **(3)** is kneeling on a rocky outcrop near the summit discussing with Capt. George Matthews **(4)** the location of the Indians below. On October 4, 1777, Matthews would suffer nine bayonet wounds while leading a regiment at the battle of Germantown. He later would be elected governor of Georgia. In the distance, smoke rising through the trees below **(5)** marks the course of fighting in the battle as the Ohio River **(6)** flows beyond. This militiaman in Matthews' company **(7)**, who thinks that he has seen an Indian, has raised his rifle to fire. Lieutenant Isaac Shelby **(8)**, now commanding his father Capt. Evan Shelby's company, has reached the same outcrop. Shelby would win fame as a commander at the battle of King's Mountain on October 7, 1780, and would later be the first governor of Kentucky. He is helping his friend Sgt. James Robertson **(9)**, who is leading the men of Shelby's company up the ridge. Robertson and Lt. John Sevier of Capt. William Russell's company would be remembered as the fathers of Tennessee.

line, a small run had eroded the high ridge's incline. There Shelby's, Stuart's, and Matthews's companies could climb to the high ridge's top.

To conceal their movement from Indians on the high ridge, Stuart later wrote, the Virginians "proceeded under cover of the bank of the Great Kanawha for three-quarters of a mile to the mouth of Crooked Creek, and thence along the bed of its tortuous course to their destination." As the afternoon approached its end, the three captains led their men to the top of the high ridge, and on to a position about 300yd from the Indians. The distance was too great for riflemen to target

This modern path follows the route of Shelby's, Stuart's, and Matthews' companies to the top of the high ridge. (Author's photograph)

individual warriors, who were also concealed by the canopy of leaves above them. But the Virginians, Stuart recalled, "poured a destructive fire on the Indian rear, and they believing that this was the long-expected reinforcement, under Colonel Christian, gave way, falling back toward the place from which they came that morning."

As night approached, the Virginians watched cautiously as the flashes from Indian muskets diminished and the shouts of the Indian warriors dwindled to silence. "An hour by sun," Todd remembered, "we were in full possession of the field of battle." Lewis then ordered his men to retire to the camp. "Victory having now declared in our favor," Todd recalled, "We had orders to return in slow pace to our camp, carefully searching for the dead and wounded to bring them in, as also the scalps of the enemy."

The Virginians collected 32 scalps, which they attached to a post at the end of the point where the Kanawha and Ohio met. About 40 Indians probably died in the battle, including the Shawnee commanders Puckeshinwa and Silver Heels. About another 70 were wounded, including the Delaware war leader Buckongahelas.

But it was their own dead and wounded that mattered to the Virginians. By 6.30pm, when the last light left the sky, they were back at their heavily guarded camp. There the talk was of casualties. All were shocked by the names of the officers who had fallen. Charles Lewis and Field both were dead, and Fleming was expected to follow them. Among the captains, Buford, Robert McClanahan, Murray, Ward, and Wilson all had been killed, and Dickinson and Skidmore wounded. And when the counting was done, word spread that a fifth of the army had been lost. In all, about 80 Virginians had been killed, and another 140 wounded.

After traveling 12 miles up the Kanawha, Lewis's messengers reached Christian at 7.00pm. He and his Fincastle County Regiment companies were encamped with their herd of cattle and fleet of canoes near what is now Leon, W. Va. There they had planned to rest before marching to join Lewis's army the next day.

After leaving a small guard with the cattle and canoes, the Fincastle County Regiment commander led about 200 men forward on a five-hour night march. "We pushed on and got in about midnight," Floyd wrote to

Twenty-two years after the battle, Pvt. Walter Newman returned to the site of the Virginians' camp. There he built this 1796 tavern overlooking the Ohio River, now the Mansion House Museum at Tu-Endie-Wei/Point Pleasant Battlefield State Park. (Photograph by Ed Lowe)

Preston, "where we were warmly received. And I imagine that if our number had been double what we were, we should not have been complained of for that. I understand we were much prayed for that day in time of the engagement... Some gentlemen tell me that it appeared doubtful for some time."

FROM POINT PLEASANT TO FORT GOWER

On October 11, Lewis's men awoke early, expecting the Indians to attack again. After hours passed without shots being fired, Lewis sent Christian's Fincastle County companies up the Ohio to search for enemy warriors. After following the tracks of the retreating Indians to the river, they found the Indians' rafts on the other side. The Virginians then spent the day burying the bodies of the Southern Army's dead.

The men at Dunmore's camp also rose early on October 11. After telling Lewis that he would advance on October 13, the impatient Virginia governor had again changed his mind. The day before, as the battle had raged, his army had crossed the Ohio. Watercraft had carried 1,400 men and 250,000lb of flour as 200 packhorses and 100 cattle had swum across the stream.

Established in 1764, Assisink was at the site of the Standing Stone, a 200ft-high outcrop of rock. The photograph shows an exposed portion, in what is now Rising Park in Lancaster, Ohio. (Author's photograph)

After resting at their 1st Ohio Camp beside the fort, the Northern Army now would march to the Pickaway Plains. Leaving 100 men to garrison the fort, about 1,300 went forward. White Eyes and Captain Pipe, worried about conflict between Dunmore's men and Indians who were not hostile, agreed to accompany them. The route to the Pickaway Plains, they knew, would pass near Assisink, a Delaware village.

Girty, Kenton, McCulloch, and a corps of the most capable scouts in the wilderness led the way. The Indians watching the army's progress soon learned not to be careless. Girty, who detected one hiding 200yd away, felled him with a rifle shot. After crossing the Ohio Ridge Trail, which led to opposite the mouth of the Kanawha, the Virginians moved cautiously up the Hocking to the mouth of Federal Creek. There, after 11 miles, they halted at their 2nd Ohio Camp, near present Beebe.

Early on October 12, Lewis dispatched James Fowler and two other scouts up the Ohio to the Virginia governor with an account of the battle. Dunmore's army, he urged, should now join his at Point Pleasant, where its physicians and medical supplies were desperately needed. That day the Northern Army advanced another 15 miles, to its 3rd Ohio Camp, near what is now Chauncey. On October 13, as Fowler and the other scouts raced up the Ohio in record time, the Virginians on the Hocking resumed their march. After 9 miles, they crossed to the river's north bank, where they halted at their 4th Ohio Camp.

After crossing the Hocking River behind these trees, Dunmore's army climbed to high ground here, where a monument in Nelsonville commemorates the site of Dunmore's 4th Ohio Camp. (Photograph by Mike Martin)

Early on October 14, Fowler arrived at Dunmore's 4th Ohio Camp. But the Virginia governor would not alter his plans. After sending Lewis a message congratulating him on his victory, Dunmore ordered his army to resume its advance. After 12 miles, it halted at its 5th Ohio Camp, at present-day Logan. That day, as the despairing Indians were nearing the Shawnee villages on the Pickaway Plains, Lewis selected new officers to command the companies whose captains had fallen. Slaughter's company then arrived with 300 cattle and the flour needed for the Southern Army's further advance. Fowler, Lewis calculated, would be back at Point Pleasant by Monday, October 17. On that day, the Southern Army would cross the Ohio. If Fowler had not returned by October 18, it would march to the Pickaway Plains alone.

On October 15, as some of Lewis's men searched the surrounding woods for horses that had fled from the camp during the battle, others began building a crude fortification where the wounded would remain. All were hopeful that Fowler would return with good news. "There are many shot in two places," Christian wrote that day to Preston, "Some in three. They are really in a deplorable situation, bad doctors, nothing to dress with proper makes it still worse… Perhaps humanity," Christian added, "will induce him to return and come to us if he is found a little way off, as Col. Lewis earnestly begged he would do so by Fowler. But should he not, our wounded must be done with the best we can. And if we don't hear more from him before, we shall march on Tuesday morning with about 12 days provisions."

But Dunmore's army was continuing to advance. At what is now Rockbridge State Nature Preserve, it reached the Belpre Trail, which the Virginians followed west to its intersection with the Standing Stone Trail on

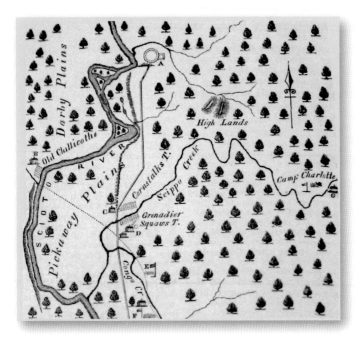

This map from Henry Howe's 1848 *Historical Collections of Ohio* shows the Pickaway Plains. Locations marked on it include: (A) earthworks left by the prehistoric Ohio "Moundbuilders" at modern Circleville; (B) Logan's cabin near Kispoko (Old Chillicothe); (E) the point where Dunmore stopped Lewis's advancing army; and (F) the site of Lewis's 7th Ohio Camp. (Author's collection)

Clear Creek. There, after a 15-mile march, they halted at their 6th Ohio Camp, in what is now Clear Creek Metropark.

Eighteen miles ahead on the Belpre Trail, the Shawnee and Mingo chiefs gathered at a council house near Grenadier Squaw's Town to decide what to do. They had failed, Cornstalk told the chiefs, to defeat Lewis's army. Should they now, he asked, attack Dunmore's? No one responded. "Let us kill all our women and children," he then proposed, "and go and fight till we die." When silence again followed, Cornstalk said that the Indians now must beg for peace. Despite the war, the Pennsylvania trader Matthew Elliott had remained on the Pickaway Plains with his Shawnee wife and two sons. Cornstalk now asked him to go to the Virginia governor.

Early on October 16, Elliott arrived at Dunmore's 6th Ohio Camp. The Shawnee and Mingos, he told Dunmore, wanted a peace council. The delighted Virginia commander then sent Girty and Gibson back to the Indians with Elliott to confirm the information. Later that day, they returned to report that the offer was genuine. The Indian chiefs, they said, had promised to send emissaries for peace negotiations at Dunmore's camp on Clear Creek. Dunmore then sent Elliott back to tell the Indians that the council would be held nearer the Shawnee villages, at a camp on Scippo Creek.

That same day, Lewis chose the officers and men who would advance to the Pickaway Plains. Fleming, whose condition was improving, would remain with three captains, who would organize new companies as wounded men recovered. Lockridge would create a new company from the Augusta County men. Slaughter would form one from the Culpeper County wounded, and those from Buford's Bedford and Pauling's Botetourt companies. Herbert would form one from the rest of the Botetourt and Fincastle companies. The remainder of the army, its casualties replaced by Christian's companies, would go forward to fight again. "Nothing," Isaac Shelby wrote his uncle that day, "can save us from another battle unless they attack the governor's party."

On Monday, October 17, about 1,125 Virginians, 120 packhorses, and 120 cattle crossed the river to the Southern Army's 1st Ohio Camp, directly across the Ohio River from the battlefield. "We had more than every fifth man in our army killed or wounded in the battle," recalled Stuart, "but none was disheartened. We crossed the river fully determined to destroy the enemy, with cheerfulness, and had they not been restrained by the Governor's orders, I believe they would have exterminated the Shawnee nation."

As Lewis's army crossed the river, the Northern Army marched 12 miles west to Scippo Creek. There, about 6 miles from Grenadier Squaw's Town, Dunmore's men halted at their 7th Ohio Camp. It would, the Virginia commander decided, be named for his wife, the Countess of Dunmore. Soon men nailed a large piece of bark to a tree, and chalked on it in red letters

"Camp Charlotte." On October 18, as Dunmore's men began building council houses for the treaty negotiations, Lewis abandoned hopes of Fowler's return. After transporting more cattle across the Ohio, he led his men forward 6 miles to their 2nd Ohio Camp.

On October 19, the peace negotiations began. Most of the raiding, the Shawnees told Dunmore, had been the work of Logan and his warriors. But the Mingo chief, Clark noticed, was not among the Indians at the negotiations. He was, the Indians said, at a cabin near Kispoko, about 9 miles from Camp Charlotte. Occupied until recently by Chalawgatha Shawnees, the town was known to the Virginians as Chillicothe.

Indians, Clark remembered, went from the council to ask Logan to attend. When they returned, they reported that the Mingo had told them that he "was like a mad dog, that his bristles had been up and were not yet quite fallen – but that the good talks now going forward might allay them." Dunmore then asked Girty and Gibson to find him.

The 104ft-high elm tree where Logan and Gibson talked survived until 1964. This monument is at the site, now Logan Elm State Memorial. (Author's photograph)

Thomas Jefferson's 1785 *Notes on the State of Virginia* made Logan's words famous. "I may challenge," he wrote, "the whole orations of Demosthenes and Cicero … to produce a single passage superior to the speech." Jefferson reproduced Logan's words as they appeared in this copy of Gibson's transcript, which he had obtained from Revolutionary War Brig. Gen. Hugh Mercer, a friend of Stephen. (Library of Congress, Manuscripts Division)

Girty made little effort to find the Mingo, who, he complained, was "a surly fellow," who might attack an uninvited emissary. Girty's concern was well founded. Logan usually appeared friendly. But when the missionary David McClure saw Logan on September 16, 1772, he thought that the Indian had considered killing him. On July 20, 1773, when Gibson was guiding the missionary John Lacey to Logan's village at the mouth of the Beaver River, Gibson learned that Logan was threatening to kill him. By the time they got to the village, Lacey wrote in his journal, the Indians "had Logan shut up in a house. Logan broke down the door, and came to us in very good humor, expressing sorrow for what he had said."

Gibson found the Mingo on Congo Creek, talking with other Indians. After the massacre of the rest of Logan's family, the settlers had taken his infant niece to Gibson, her father. When Gibson had joined Dunmore's army, he had left her at his trading post, where he would raise her. When Logan, who did not know that his niece had survived, begun crying when he saw Gibson. He then led the trader to a nearby elm tree, where he addressed Gibson in English.

The Mingo's words so moved the trader that, when he returned to Camp Charlotte, he wrote them down. Because of the killing at Baker's trading post, Logan had ended his speech, "There runs not a drop of my blood in the veins of any living creature. This called on me for revenge. I have sought it. I have killed many. I have fully glutted my vengeance. For my country I rejoice at the beams of peace. But do not harbor a thought that mine is the joy of fear. Logan never felt fear. He will not turn on his heel to save his life. Who is there to mourn for Logan? Not one."

That day, eager to reach the Indians as quickly as possible, Lewis's men marched about 17 miles to their 3rd Ohio Camp. There they expected to be attacked at any moment. At dawn on October 20, Ens.

Lewis's 3rd Ohio Camp was near this 19th-century iron furnace in Cooper Hollow Wildlife Area, near Oak Hill. (Photograph by Red Martin)

Scippo Creek today at the site of Grenadier Squaw's Town (above the bank on the left) and Cornstalk's Town (above the bank on the right). (Author's photograph)

James Newell of Herbert's company was at the camp, preparing to return to Point Pleasant. "There was a large body of Indians seen by the scouts," he wrote in his journal, "and there was alarm in the camp. All the men turned out and formed a circle and stood about one and a half hours and no enemy appearing they marched off." The Virginians then advanced another 16 miles to where the Standing Stone Trail crossed their path. There, about 3 miles northwest of present Jackson, they halted at their 4th Ohio Camp.

On October 21, the Southern Army continued up the Kanawha Trail. After 17 miles, they halted at Walnut Creek, about 4 miles north of present-day Richmond Dale. That day, the Indians at Camp Charlotte agreed to Dunmore's treaty terms. They would return all prisoners, forego hunting beyond the Ohio River, and allow unhindered traffic on the stream. In return, no Virginians would go beyond the river except traders licensed by Dunmore. The following spring, the Ohio Indians would attend a grand council at Pittsburgh to confirm the peace agreement.

On October 22, when Lewis's men reached the Scioto Trail, a messenger from Dunmore arrived. The Northern Army, he said, was camped on Scippo Creek, where Dunmore was negotiating a peace with the Indians. After a 17-mile march, Lewis's army ended the day at their 6th Ohio Camp, in what is now the Kinnickinnick Wildlife Area.

On October 23, as Lewis's army marched up the Scioto Trail, Indians fired on the advancing Virginians. Lewis's men again halted and assumed a defensive position before resuming their advance. Indian scouts then rushed to report that Lewis's army was so close that it could reach Grenadier Squaw's Town that afternoon.

When the alarmed Indians told Dunmore, the Virginia governor dispatched another a messenger to the Southern Army commander. The Indians, he informed Lewis, had now agreed to his peace terms. Lewis was to encamp his army and await further orders. His men, the skeptical Southern Army commander responded, would stop at the next good campsite. They found it on Congo Creek. There they halted at their 7th Ohio Camp, about 2 miles south of Grenadier Squaw's Town, and 7 miles from Camp Charlotte.

These Indian artifacts, an iron pan with 3ft-long handle and copper kettle, were unearthed in 2013 at the site of the Burning Ground. (Jeff Dearth Collection)

On the morning of October 24, yet another messenger from Dunmore arrived. The Virginia governor, Lewis later told Fleming, had sent him to invite Lewis "and any officers he thought proper" to come to Camp Charlotte, But, Lewis said, he had not thought it "prudent to go to his lordship's camp with only two or three officers and therefore marched thereto with a design to join his lordship."

When Indian scouts saw the Virginians beginning to form columns, they reported that Lewis's army was about to attack the Shawnee towns. As Dunmore and Gibson raced to intercept the Southern Army, Lewis's men marched up the Scioto Trail past the site where Logan and Gibson had talked. Beyond Congo Creek, a small trail to Camp Charlotte diverged to the right. But the Southern Army, Christian recalled, "passed the path that led to our right hand." "His guide," Lewis told Fleming, "mistook the path."

Dunmore's and Gibson's fear was well founded. Although Lewis's men had not marched to attack the Indians, they were approaching sights that would enrage them. Some, like 26-year-old Pvt. George See of Arbuckle's company, had seen them before. In 1763, he had been captured with his mother, two brothers, and four sisters. Though the Shawnees had freed the others in 1765, his 11-year-old sister Elizabeth had never been returned.

Just ahead, See knew, was where four old Shawnee women greeted the warriors returning with captives. Their lips smeared with red clay to make them look like drinkers of blood, they chose the prisoners who would be ritually eaten. To the right would be the 7ft-wide, 300yd-long, gauntlet course, where the captives ran while they were whipped. And to the left, the small hill the Virginians called the "Burning Ground," where the lives of many settlers had ended in flames.

Just before Lewis's men entered the area, Dunmore and Gibson reached them. The Virginia commander then ordered Lewis to lead his men back to their 7th Ohio Camp. That evening Dunmore arrived at the camp with a 50-man escort.

When the Virginia governor reached Lewis's tent, the Southern Army commander later told his son, his men were so furious with Dunmore that he had to treble the usual guard. He had not intended to disobey the Virginia governor's orders, he told his commander. Nor would his men attack the Indians now that there was peace. Dunmore then, after thanking the Southern Army's officers for their service, ordered Lewis to lead his men back to Camp Union.

The view today from the Burning Ground, looking south toward Congo Creek. Dunmore halted Lewis's army behind the first line of trees in the center. (Author's photograph)

On October 25, the Southern Army departed for Point Pleasant, where the men whose blood had purchased Dunmore's peace remained. Andrew Lewis and William Christian, Isaac Shelby and Thomas Posey, James Harrod and James Robertson, John Floyd and John Todd and the rest, all then marched through present Chillicothe, Jackson, and Gallipolis toward fields where they soon would fight more battles. Only Russell and his men stayed behind. After marching to Fort Gower, they were to build a permanent

Captured after the June 4–5, 1782 battle of Upper Sandusky, Crawford would be tortured to death by Captain Pipe's Delawares. This statue of Crawford is at the site of his fort, now Connellsville, Pa. (Photograph by Ed Lowe)

stronghold at the mouth of the Kanawha. It was to be named Fort Blair after other of Dunmore's titles, Baron Murray of Blair.

Not all of the Indians, however, had agreed to the Virginia governor's peace terms. As Lewis's men were leaving their camp on Congo Creek, Dunmore learned that the Mingos were gathering at Seekunk, 30 miles up the Scioto. On October 27, they would move north to new villages near Lake Erie, taking with them the prisoners, horses, and goods they had captured in raids.

The Scioto River, as seen from the site of Seekunk, now Dodge Park in downtown Columbus. (Photograph by Wendy S. Winkler)

Dunmore sent Crawford and 240 men to stop them. Afraid that the Shawnees would warn the Mingos, he told them that the Virginians were leaving to escort a resupply convoy from Fort Gower. That evening Crawford led Cresap's, Clark's, Aston's, and Daniel Morgan's companies back toward Clear Creek. Then, guided by Girty, they turned to the northwest up Salt Creek.

On October 26, they moved undetected across Little Walnut and then Big Walnut creeks toward the Scioto. When they began to approach Seekunk the following night, Crawford divided his force. Two companies formed a semicircle around Seekunk, which they would attack at dawn on October 27. The other two moved a half-mile north. When they heard gunfire at Seekunk, they were to attack a smaller Mingo village further up the Scioto.

"Unfortunately," Crawford would write to Washington on November 14, "one of our men was discovered by the Indians who lay out from the town at a distance... This happened before daylight, which did us much damage as a chief part of the Indians made their escape in the dark." Nonetheless, the attack was a success. "The whole of the Mingos," he wrote, "was ready to start, and was to have set off on that morning we attacked them." One of his men had been wounded, Crawford reported, but they had killed six Mingos, wounded more, and taken 14 prisoners. They had also rescued two Virginia captives, and recovered many horses and much property taken in raids.

On October 28, when Lewis's army reached Point Pleasant, the Virginia governor began preparing to return to Fort Gower as soon as Crawford's men returned. As evidence of their good faith, the Indian chiefs asked to accompany the Virginians as far as the Ohio River.

On October 31, Lewis and his men, who had had their fill and more of Virginia's royal governor, left Point Pleasant for Camp Union. That same day, Dunmore's men and the Indians began moving toward Fort Gower. On a boundless carpet of amber, golden, and russet leaves, George Rogers Clark and Daniel Morgan, John Sevier and William Crawford, Simon Girty and Simon Kenton, Adam Stephen and Matthew Elliott, Michael Cresap and John Gibson, Cornstalk and Nonhelema, Blue Jacket and Black Hoof,

The view today from the site of Fort Gower, showing the Hocking River (right) flowing into the Ohio (ahead). (Photograph by Mike Murdoch)

White Eyes and Captain Pipe and many more who would become legends, marched together in the greatest of frontier parades.

At their head was a triumphant Dunmore, now lord of the woods. Master of the western savages, Indians and frontier settlers alike, he had equaled Bouquet's achievement and secured for Virginia the American West. Hundreds of new settlements, he foresaw, soon would extend down the Ohio to the Mississippi, and across Kentucky. And he would become fabulously rich.

The thoughts of Dunmore's officers, however, were elsewhere. The Indian war over, they talked of what might have happened in Boston and Philadelphia while they had been west of the Appalachians. And also of what now might come.

The 2,400 riflemen who had camped on the Scippo and Congo Creeks had been a formidable force. Such men had fought before in British armies. But these men had not been in British armies. They had been in Virginia armies. Or perhaps, Dunmore's officers concluded, American armies. As they passed through the sites of present Logan and Nelsonville, Chauncey and Athens, Daniel Morgan later wrote, "We formed ourselves into a society and pledged our word of honor to each other to assist our brethren of Boston in case hostilities should commence."

When the Virginians reached Fort Gower, the Indians departed. Dunmore's officers then assembled on November 5 to discuss the conflict with Britain. Before leaving to follow their different paths towards home, they voted unanimously to publish a joint statement in Virginia's newspaper, the *Virginia Gazette*.

"We have lived about three months in the woods without any intelligence from Boston, or from the delegates at Philadelphia," began what would be remembered as the Fort Gower Resolves. If there was to be war with Britain, it continued, the Americans would have an army. "That we are a respectable body is certain when it is considered that we can live weeks without bread or salt, that we can sleep in the open air without any covering but that of the canopy of heaven, and that our men can march and shoot with any in the known world." And, it ended, "We resolve that we will exert every power within us for the defense of American liberty."

THE AFTERMATH

When Dunmore returned to Williamsburg on December 4, he learned that his new daughter had been born the day before. But the other news was bad. On September 22, when Lewis had reached his 12th W. Va. Camp, the Continental Congress had asked American merchants to cease purchasing British goods. On October 15, the day Dunmore had reached his 5th Ohio Camp, it had issued a Declaration of Colonial Rights. On October 20, when Lewis had reached his 4th Ohio Camp, it had voted to create the American Association, a permanent league of the 13 colonies. And on October 26, as Crawford had marched north to Seekunk, it had dissolved with an announcement that it would reconvene on May 10, 1775 unless the British government repealed its intolerable legislation.

On December 22, the Fort Gower Resolves appeared in the *Virginia Gazette* like a thunderbolt in the western sky. It was the first public announcement that, if the British did not satisfy the colonists' grievances, they would face an American army. Lewis's Southern Army officers soon issued joint statements expressing their approval.

At the same time, Boston newspapers were contrasting the militiamen who had fought at Point Pleasant with the British regulars who occupied their town. "The professed design of Britain in maintaining standing armies in America," wrote one, "was the protection of the colonies." But none of the 7,000 British soldiers in America had marched west to fight the Indians. "The battle between the brave Virginians and their savage neighbors," it continued, showed that the colonies

The Dec. 22, 1774 issue of the *Virginia Gazette* contained the Fort Gower Resolves (beginning lower right). (Courtesy of the Virginia Historical Society).

THE CULPEPER MINUTE MEN

LIBERTY OR DEATH

DONT TREAD ON ME

A year after Col. John Field fell at Point Pleasant, his Culpeper County militiamen fought under this banner at Great Bridge. The engraving is from Benson Lossing's *Popular Cyclopedia of United States History.* (Author's collection)

"are able and willing to defend themselves… The real design of keeping a standing army in America," it ominously concluded, "was not protecting but enslaving the colonies."

After Seekunk, the Mingos remained hostile to the Virginians, but Logan went on no more raids. The Shawnees, moreover, honored their agreement by returning captives to Fort Blair. In 1775, they brought John Field's son Ezekiel, who had, he reported, been "treated cruelly" and William Robinson, whom Logan had saved from the Burning Ground. George See's sister Elizabeth, now 20, returned as well, leaving behind with the Shawnees a four-year-old son and two-year-old daughter. And so did others, such as 15-year-old Richard Sparks, who would in time command the US Army's 2nd Infantry Regiment.

In March, when the Fort Gower Resolves were read aloud in the House of Commons to outraged members of Parliament, the settlement of Kentucky began. On March 8, Harrod and his men began the long journey back to their abandoned cabins in Harrodsburg, Kentucky's first settlement. On March 18, Boone and 31 axemen began blazing the Wilderness Trail through the Cumberland Gap. Tens of thousands of Virginians would follow them to Boonesborough and other Kentucky settlements.

As Harrod's and Boone's settlers went west, Americans east of the Appalachians waited in vain for good news from Britain. On March 28, Dunmore issued a proclamation forbidding the election of Virginia delegates to attend the Continental Congress when it reconvened. Protesting Virginians, led by Patrick Henry, threatened to use the colony's militia to prevent its enforcement. "I once fought for the Virginians," an angry Dunmore responded, "but, by God, I would let them see that I could fight against them."

Then the fighting began. On April 19, when Gage attempted to repeat his seizure of Massachusetts militia arsenals, more than 300 British soldiers and American militiamen were killed or wounded at Lexington and Concord. When the news reached Virginia on April 29, 150 Hanover County militiamen, led by Henry, marched on Williamsburg. On May 6, Dunmore and his family fled. When the news reached Hannastown on May 16, St. Clair and others gathered at the courthouse, where they issued the Hannastown Resolves, the first published call for Americans to form an army to fight the British.

On July 3, Washington arrived in Cambridge, Mass., where the Continental Army had been assembled to drive the British from Boston. Waiting to greet the army's commander were Cresap and 150 riflemen waiting, who had marched more than 500 miles to greet him. On August 8, Daniel Morgan arrived with 96 more.

To suppress the rebellion in Virginia, Britain's royal governor tried to use the Ohio Indians. At Dunmore's request, Connolly sent a letter to White Eyes, asking him to lead the Ohio Indians against the western settlers. But the puzzled Delaware chief showed it to John Gibson. When news of the letter spread, St Clair and an army of furious frontiersmen took control of Pittsburgh.

Connolly fled to Virginia, where Dunmore had assembled an army of British soldiers and American loyalists that was fighting to retain control of the colony. But on December 9, the rifles of Culpeper County militiamen defeated them at the battle of Great Bridge. Continental Army soldiers led by Andrew Lewis and Adam Stephen then drove Dunmore from his last Virginia base at the battle of Gwynn's Island on July 9, 1776.

During the Revolutionary War, Butler, Clark, Lewis, Daniel Morgan, Posey, St Clair, and Stephen all would become American generals. Christian, Crawford, Gibson and Matthews would command regiments. Campbell, Sevier and Isaac Shelby would win fame as commanders of militia forces.

For a time, it was uncertain whether the war would spread west of the Appalachians. On March 2, 1776, as Americans were considering independence, White Eyes addressed the Continental Congress. He would try, he said, to form a union of the Ohio Indians, which Congress should recognize as the 14th state of the new United States.

For two years, while the British debated whether to seek the aid of the Ohio Indians, the Mingos battled the Americans alone. On Christmas Day, 1776, Pluggy and 30 warriors attacked Harrod's new settlement, and a nearby party led by John Todd. But three days later, the Mingo chief fell fighting.

After leaving Virginia, Dunmore returned to Dunmore Park, his estate near Airth in Scotland. His summerhouse at the estate, known as The Pineapple, survives to this day. (Author's collection)

Many prominent British leaders, including William Pitt, who had been prime minister during the French and Indian War, thought that British use of the Indians against the Americans would be shameful. But in June 1777, the commandant at British Fort Detroit received orders to urge the Ohio Indians to attack American settlements.

Events then favored the British. On November 10, 1777, Indians killed a militiaman near Fort Randolph, which had been built at Point Pleasant to replace Fort Blair. Infuriated soldiers at the fort then killed Cornstalk, who was visiting on a peace mission. On March 27, 1778, McKee, Girty, and Elliott fled from Pittsburgh to join the British. McKee, as chief British agent among the Ohio Indians, and Elliott, as his deputy, would guide the actions of Britain's Indian allies during the Revolutionary War. Girty, who would lead the Indians in many engagements, would become the most hated man on the frontier.

By the end of 1778, White Eyes was dead, and most of the Ohio Indians had joined the British. But by then, thousands of settlers had emigrated to Kentucky. Fighting of unsurpassed brutality raged, in which the dead included Crawford, Floyd, and Todd. But the Kentuckians, led by Clark, prevailed in campaigns that allowed the United States at the end of the Revolutionary War to claim borders that extended to the Great Lakes and the Mississippi River.

Aided covertly by McKee and Elliott, the Ohio Indians fought on without the British, first against Kentucky militiamen, and then against soldiers of the new US Army. In 1791, when St Clair became the US Army's commanding general, he led it against the Ohio Indians. At Wabash, they destroyed his army and killed Butler, his second in command. But in 1794, a reborn US Army, commanded by Maj. Gen. Anthony Wayne, defeated them at Fallen Timbers.

Sixteen years of peace followed, during which Ohio became a state and Indiana, Illinois, and Michigan territories. Then Puckeshinwa's sons the Prophet and Tecumseh renewed the fighting, first at the 1811 battle of Tippecanoe and then during the War of 1812. Thirty-nine years after Point Pleasant, it finally ended at the 1813 battle of the Thames. There an army of Americans and allied Indians, including 1,000 Kentucky volunteers led by Isaac Shelby, and 150 Shawnees led by Black Hoof, destroyed a British and Indian army, killed Tecumseh, and brought a permanent peace to the Ohio Country.

THE BATTLEFIELD TODAY

Museums, parks and monuments are at the sites of many significant events during Lord Dunmore's War. A marker in the rest area on Ohio Route 113 near Yellow Creek, Ohio, commemorates Logan's camp. Another, on W. Va. Route 2 near Waterford Park, is near the site of Baker's trading post. The site of Fort Dunmore is now the Fort Pitt Museum in Point State Park in Pittsburgh. A marker on Main Street between 10th and 11th streets in Wheeling, W. Va., is at the site of Fort Fincastle, renamed Fort Henry during the Revolutionary War. Wakatomica was in Dresden, Ohio, and the battle of that name 6 miles to the south, east of the intersection of Ohio Route 666 and Memory Road.

Andrew Lewis's Fort Lewis was in Salem, Va., where the Salem Museum and Historical Society, at 801 E. Main Street, has exhibits on Lewis's life. Camp Union was in downtown Lewisburg, W. Va. Markers tracing the course of Lewis's march are at the intersections of US Route 60 and Brushy Ridge Rd. near Alta; US Route 60 and W. Va. Route 14, about 5 miles southeast of Lookout; US Route 60 and County Road 81 in Cedar Grove; and US Route 60 and Veazy Street in Charleston; on Fairlawn Ave at Shawnee Regional Park in Institute; and in a park beside W. Va. Route 2, just south of Hometown.

The site of the battle is now Point Pleasant, W. Va, where Tu-Endie-Wei/ Point Pleasant Battlefield State Park occupies an area of the Virginia camp. There visitors will find the Mansion House Museum, the graves of Cornstalk and Mad Ann Bailey, and many monuments. The nearby River Walk leads up the Ohio past murals depicting scenes from the battle. A reproduction of Fort Randolph is in Krodel Park.

Fort Gower was at the end of Pearl Street in Hockingport, Ohio. A monument in Nelsonville, at the intersection of US Route 33, and Pine Grove Drive, is near the site of Dunmore's 4th Ohio Camp. Another near Leistville, on Ohio Route 56, half a mile north of Ohio Route 159, is at the site of Camp Charlotte. A marker 4 miles south of Circleville, on Emerson Road, nearly a half-mile east of US Route 23, is near

The battlefield today. (Author's map)

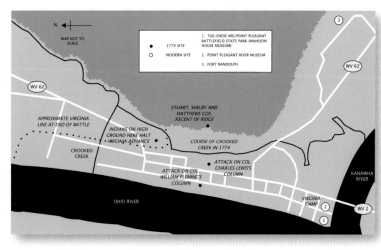

93

the location of Grenadier Squaw's Town, Cornstalk's Town and the Burning Ground. The site of Logan's speech is now Logan Elm State Memorial, a park on Ohio Route 361, a mile east of US Route 23, where many monuments commemorate figures in Lord Dunmore's War. Seekunk was in downtown Columbus, in Dodge Park on Sullivant Avenue.

In 1776, militiamen led by Capt. Matthew Arbuckle built Fort Randolph to replace Fort Blair. On May 16–18, 1778, Wyandots besieged the stronghold, which has been reconstructed in Point Pleasant. (Photograph by Ed Lowe)

FURTHER READING

Booth, Russell H., *The Tuscarawas Valley in Indian Days, 1750–1797* (1994)
De Haas, Wills, *History of the Early Settlement and Indian Wars of Western Virginia* (1851)
Downes, Randolph C., "Dunmore's War: an Interpretation" in *The Mississippi Valley Historical Review*, Vol. 21, No. 3 (Dec., 1934), pp. 311–330 (Urbana, Ill., 1934)
Hammon, Neal O., and Taylor, Richard, *Virginia's Western Wars, 1775–1786* (2002)
Hintzen, William, *The Border Wars of the Upper Ohio Valley, 1769–1794* (1999)
Howard, James A., *Shawnee: The Ceremonialism of a Native American Tribe and its Cultural Background* (1981)
Hoffman, Phillip W., *Simon Girty: Turncoat Hero* (2008)
Kercheval, Samuel, *A History of the Valley of Virginia* (1833)
Lewis, Vergil A., *History of the Battle of Point Pleasant* (1909)
McConnell, Michael N., *A Country Between, the Upper Ohio Valley and its Peoples, 1724–1774* (1992)
Meyer, Brantz, *Tah-Gah-Jute; or, Logan and Cresap, An Historical Essay* (1867)
Safford, William H., "An Outing on the Congo: A Visit to the Site of Dunmore's Treaty with the Shawnee in 1774" in *Ohio Archaeological and Historical Society Quarterly*, Vol. 7, pp. 349–366 (Columbus, 1898)
Simpson-Poffenbarger, Livia N., *The Battle of Point Pleasant, A Battle of the Revolution, October I0th, 1774, Biographical Sketches of the Men Who Participated* (1909)
Skidmore, Warren, and Kaminsky, Donna, *Lord Dunmore's Little War of 1774: His Captains and the Men Who Opened Up Kentucky and the West to American Settlements* (2002)
Smith, James, *An Account of the Remarkable Occurrences in the Life and Travels of Colonel James Smith* (1907)
Smyth, Cecil B., *Dunmore's War 1774, a Concise Narrative of the 1774 Campaign of the Virginia Frontiersmen Against the Indian Tribes of the Ohio Valley* (1993)
Stuart, John, "Narrative by Captain John Stuart of General Andrew Lewis's Expedition Against the Indians in the Year 1774 and of the Battle of Point Pleasant, Virginia" in *Magazine of American History*, Vol. 11, Part 1 (Nov., 1877), pp. 668–679 (New York, 1877)
Sugden, John, *Blue Jacket* (2000)
Tanner, Helen H., *Atlas of Great Lakes Indian History* (1986)
Thwaites, Reuben G., "Cornstalk" in *Ohio Archaeological and Historical Society Quarterly*, Vol. 21, pp. 345–362 (Columbus, 1912).
Thwaites, Reuben G., and Kellogg, Louise P., *Documentary History of Dunmore's War, 1774* (1905)

INDEX